Praise for *Mon...*

"Macks, a longtime writer for *The Tonight Show with Jay Leno* . . . examines not only what makes something funny, but also how a joke can help shape public opinion and public behavior and what constitutes inappropriate material. . . . Readers looking for some behind-the-scenes intel on the big stars and the popular late-night shows won't be disappointed. . . . Without Jon Stewart on late night, fans may need something else to do: this book should help." —*Booklist*

"Jon Macks is one of the funniest and most prolific comedy writers I have worked with. Like a great pitcher, he has a dazzling arsenal of fastballs and curves. Whether it's politics or pop culture, he gets it instantly. And everything he says about me in *Monologue* is true." —Billy Crystal

"Jon Macks is a brilliant craftsman who provides a spectacular insider's view of how the writers do the work and we clowns take the credit." —Martin Short

"After more than twenty years writing for *The Tonight Show with Jay Leno*, Jon Macks knows what makes a great host and a great guest, a good joke from a bad one, and how to keep the audience at home up past bedtime. In *Monologue*, he tells the stories behind the stories and proves that late-night TV is still the place where public opinion is formed." —James Carville

"Jon Macks is one of the greatest comedy writers of all time. Just like Billy Preston worked behind the scenes with the Beatles and the Stones, Macks has been the man behind so many great comedians it's impossible to name them all. I'm proud to say there is no comedic situation I'll ever enter without him."

—Chris Rock

"After writing 500,000 jokes for Jay Leno, Jon Macks has written a funny and fascinating book about late-night TV. He is the Cal Ripken Jr. of comedy, turning in an all-star quality performance for two decades. *Monologue* tells you how he did it, and reminds us all of why we love to laugh in bed."

—Paul Begala

"More than one A-list star has dubbed Jon Macks 'the Joke Machine,' a nickname that's well-earned. Chances are you already know some of his most memorable lines, because he's written them for everyone, from the Beltway to Hollywood and back. If you don't believe me, just read this book. If you do believe me, read it anyway. He owes me money."   —Dave Boone

ALSO BY JON MACKS

How to Be Funny

*Fugheddaboutit: How to Badda Boom, Badda
Bing, and Find Your Inner Mobster*

From Soup to Nuts: The Cannibal Lover's Cookbook

Heaven Talks Back

Monologue

WHAT MAKES AMERICA LAUGH BEFORE BED

Jon Macks

BLUE RIDER PRESS

Penguin Random House

New York

To Jay Leno, to anyone who writes or who has ever written a late-night monologue joke, and to all the late-night hosts. They are the people who make us laugh before going to bed.

blue
rider
press

BLUE RIDER PRESS
An imprint of Penguin Random House LLC
375 Hudson Street
New York, New York 10014

The Library of Congress has catalogued the hardcover edition as follows:

Macks, Jon.
Monologue : what makes America laugh before bed / Jon Macks.
p.   cm.
ISBN 978-0-399-17166-6 (hardcover)
1. Television talk shows—United States.   2. Macks, Jon.   3. Television comedy writers—United States—Biography.   I. Title.
PN1992.8.T3M33   2015   2015002605
791.45'6—dc23

Blue Rider Press hardcover: April 2015
Blue Rider Press paperback: April 2016
Blue Rider Press paperback ISBN: 978-0-399-18340-9

Printed in the United States of America
1   3   5   7   9   10   8   6   4   2

BOOK DESIGN BY NICOLE LAROCHE

FOREWORD

A lot has happened to me since Jay Leno's *Tonight Show* went off the air and this book was first published.

For starters, I finally got to meet Mel Brooks. Mel was set to present the comedy series award at the 67th Emmy Awards, and he wanted to talk to me about writing an opening line. A call was arranged and after we talked for a few minutes and worked out how he would open his talk, Mel said, "Macks? What is that?"

I said, "Jewish."

He asked, "What was the name originally?"

I said, "Take your pick, my grandparents were Polavansky, Buten, Goldberg, and Breilof."

He said, "When we meet in person, I'm calling you Polavansky."

Of course he would, it's a funnier name. We chatted for a minute more. He wanted to know how I'd gotten started, asked about some mutual friends, and then he said, "And in my dressing room I want an egg salad sandwich—no, make that two."

Wait a second, I'm an eight-time Emmy nominee. Who is Mel Brooks to ask me to get him an egg sal— Wait, he's an EGOT. An Emmy, Grammy, Oscar, and Tony winner. There are more people who have been elected president than who have won an EGOT. There are about the same number of people with EGOTs as the number of people who walked on the moon. Although I did find out there are more EGOTs than actual women on the Ashley Madison website. I think the latest numbers are twenty million men and three women. Three very busy women. The point is, Mel is a real legend and a real mensch.

I made sure Mel had his egg salad.

In June 2015, I went to Israel for the second awarding of the Genesis Prize, given to an individual who has attained excellence in his or her chosen field and who exemplifies Jewish values. Jay Leno was the emcee again, and this time the recipient was Michael Douglas. I write for both Jay and Michael and also do some work for Genesis. At lunch the day before the ceremony, the table included Jay, Michael, Catherine Zeta-Jones, coaching legend Pat Riley, and me. Everyone who walked by stared at us. Everyone in Israel seemed to know these superstars. You could almost hear them saying to themselves: "That's Jay Leno; that's Michael Douglas; oh my God, it's Catherine Zeta-Jones, and Pat Riley, too. Who is the guy with them?" One older woman came up to me at the table and said, "Congratulations, you must be their agent."

I got to work on an AFI Tribute for one of my comedy heroes, Steve Martin, and work with another one of my comedy heroes, Martin Short. A few months later I had dinner with Marty, and at the tables next to us were Larry David with David Steinberg; Ricky Gervais and Kevin Pollak with Christopher Guest; and then there was Marty and me. The waitress took one look at Marty, Ricky, Larry, Kevin, and Christopher, all comedy geniuses, then looked at me, and said, "You must be their agent."

And I got to check one off the bucket list when I was interviewed by Chuck Todd on *Meet the Press*. I've always been a fan of Chuck's, and being able to sit in that studio was fantastic. After the interview Chuck walked me to the door, and I could see through the glass the limo driver staring at me in obvious admiration: Who is that handsome star talking to Mr. Todd? As I got in the car he turned to me and said, "So, you must be Chuck's agent."

I also got to work on a Michael Bublé Christmas special, with a cameo by Miss Piggy, the very same Miss Piggy who I once hung up on John Kerry for. I find it ironic that while John was negotiating with Jews and Muslims, I was busy talking to pork. And there were things I didn't do this past year. I didn't get drugged by Bill Cosby, I'm too male; I didn't get propositioned by Jared from Subway, I'm too old; and I didn't get to go to a strip club with Josh Duggar, I'm too Jewish.

But a lot more has happened to the world of late night in a year. We bid farewell to Jon Stewart and David Letterman, witnessed the seismic shift their departures caused, not just in the dynamic of late night but in changing the playing field for the wave upon wave of politicians who used these shows seeking votes and better approval ratings.

Now that we have the benefit of time and distance from Jon Stewart's last show, we can put all the adulation he got in perspective. And guess what? He deserved it and more. His influence and impact is different from that of Johnny Carson and Jay; it can't and shouldn't be measured in total viewers every night, but in the way he shaped the political debate. And for the right-wing critics, if JFK can have a reporter carry messages back and forth to the Russians during the Cuban Missile Crisis, then President Obama can go on *The Daily Show* seven times and can meet privately with Jon twice. And why not? The president's job is to deliver a message and use the bully pulpit to shape public opinion, and Jon and his show were an effective way to communicate.

As *Politico* said: "Love Stewart's jokes or hate them, he has proven to be a unique voice who is capable of turning in-the-weeds policy discussions into viral video sensations that the country is still talking about the next morning. As the White House recognized, Stewart can, at times, be a more potent influence on policy than Obama himself. The 52-year-old funnyman is widely credited with changing how the government treated military veterans and Sept. 11 first responders and for the cancellation of a hyper-partisan CNN talk show. His broadsides against President George W. Bush's Iraq War and a series of Obama missteps had a searing effect on how Americans thought about Washington."

And his unique voice is continuing with his new four-year deal at HBO. Stewart will be providing timely digital/streaming content and commentary on politics. Good news for Stewart fans; I'm guessing bad news for hypocritical candidates.

In other words, Jon is a game changer who did what all comedians do. He held up a mirror to show us what's stupid (like Jay did), and he turned a spotlight on what's wrong in Washington while making us laugh and think. On that last show on Comedy Central he said, "If you smell something, say something," and that's what the very best of all late-night hosts do.

For more than thirty years David Letterman "smelled something and said something," although it was more about the nature of TV itself. He helped define late night and gave it his own edgy, rebellious stamp. Jon influenced politics, Letterman influenced the entire next generation of late nighters. I loved his last show. My favorite line was Chris Rock's. In the final Top 10, Chris said, "I'm just glad your show is being given to another white guy."

And that white guy is Stephen Colbert. Here's my early take on Colbert. He may be the new Jack Paar, Tom Snyder, or Dick Cavett. Where the other late nighters seem to focus on really funny bits that we download and forward to one another the next day, Colbert has in his first few weeks focused on memorable interviews. It is a totally different show than what I had expected. I had originally predicted (remember, I'm also the one who predicted *Rocky 6* would win an Oscar) he would have a long and varied monologue like Jay. Instead, his most memorable moments have been with political candidates: Jeb Bush, Joe Biden, Donald Trump, Ted Cruz, and Hillary Clinton. As his show has evolved, Colbert has added a bit more edge to his interviews, sometimes being who he is in real life, a "nice guy," sometimes evoking the edge he exhibited on *The Colbert Report*. As an example, after the disastrous debate by the CNBC anchors—you remember, the one with questions a tenth grader would have been embarrassed by—Colbert devastated them in a seven-minute tour de force where the nicest thing he said was that the anchors were "unburdened by a shred of respect."

As of this writing, Jimmy Fallon continues to dominate the ratings (as I predicted), but Colbert gives viewers a real choice. If you want more of a variety show, there's Jimmy Fallon and James Corden; viral bits: Jimmy Kimmel and Jimmy Fallon; a more traditional monologue: Seth Meyers and Conan O'Brien; fascinating interviews: Colbert.

Now there is a danger for Colbert. You come out dancing and telling a few jokes and the audience expects one thing, and then you have a US senator talking about Syria as your first guest and it may be a bit confusing.

And political guests on late night have never been more prevalent. In 2016 it looks like late night's influence on our election will be bigger than ever. On one night in September there were three candidates on the late-night shows. Ted Cruz went on *Colbert*, Carly Fiorina went on *Fallon*, and Bernie Sanders was on Larry Wilmore's *The Nightly Show*. And Rick Perry watched at home. Sorry, I hope I didn't offend Rick's supporter. (Think about it, he and Scott Walker were at about 1 percent of the vote. Given the margin of error of plus or minus 4 percent, they could actually have been at minus 3 percent. They could actually owe us votes.)

Trump and Jeb Bush have been on *Colbert*, Hillary has been on *Ellen* and *SNL*, and Joe Biden's appearance on *Colbert* was a defining moment in his career. We saw the Joe Biden as he really is—smart, caring, interesting, and real. Ultimately, he decided not to run for president in 2016, but that single appearance gave his prospective candidacy the fuel from which it could have launched if he had so chosen. And that gets to the heart of why late-night shows have an impact. No matter who the candidates are, when they go on a Sunday show or on *Hannity*, *Maddow*, or *O'Reilly*, they are way too calculating. They know the topic areas of the questions, they have their prepackaged answers, and it's like sex after twenty years of marriage. Everyone knows what the other person is going to do. Kate McKinnon perfectly nailed it on the *SNL* Democratic debate sketch, when as Hillary she said, "I think you're really going to like the Hillary Clinton that my team and I have created for this debate," and later when she said to "Anderson Cooper," after he asked about the e-mail scandal, "Well, Coop, I welcome this question because I rehearsed this answer the longest."

And that's what it is: rehearsed answers on Sunday shows. As a side note, that *SNL* Democratic debate sketch was not only their best piece of political comedy since Tina Fey and Amy Poehler were Sarah Palin and Hillary, but Larry David could win an Oscar if they ever cast him as Bernie in "The Bernie Sanders Story."

On a late-night show you are far more likely to see the real person, unrehearsed and unscripted. And the importance of that cannot be overstated. See, for instance, the early success of Trump and Sanders, candidates who are not political or calculating. They know who they are and we know who they are. The rest of the candidates would do well to follow what Uncle Joe did on *Colbert* and give us an unfiltered and "unfocused group" look at who they really are.

For those who wanted someone different on late night, welcome Trevor Noah. I don't think any other host speaks seven languages, comes from South Africa, or grew up under apartheid. And I don't think a host has faced a bigger challenge since Jay took over from Johnny.

Jon Stewart left his show in good hands. And I like the fact that as someone born overseas, Noah has an outsider's unique perspective on America, a tradition that goes from Alexis de Tocqueville to John Oliver. And this is a plus, because he shouldn't be a continuation of Stewart's *Daily Show*—he can't be "JS Lite," he needs to be Trevor Noah and make it his show, just like Jay had to make *The Tonight Show* his own, as did Jimmy Fallon.

So the early report card on Trevor Noah: good jokes, good comic presence, needs to work on interviews. He has a tendency to cut off guests a little too soon and doesn't yet know how to rescue an interview that is going nowhere, which is basically the same thing one can say of any other new late-night host his first few weeks.

Late-night television hosts have a double-edged responsibility: They have to acknowledge the news of the day, and they have to entertain us. I was most reminded of this when the first 2001 Emmy telecast was cancelled because of September 11. The show was rescheduled a few weeks later and Walter Cronkite was due to open the broadcast and put everything in perspective. It was about two p.m. on a Sunday and Walter was going over his copy with me. The idea was he would quote Edward R. Murrow on the higher aims of TV and talk about how entertainment can heal us.

We were about halfway through going over his remarks when he said, "Jon, we can keep doing this but the show is going to get cancelled again."

I asked why, and he said, "They just slipped me a note saying we have begun bombing Afghanistan." I was hoping he'd end that comment with "and that's the way it is," but instead he said, "We might as well finish these remarks." We did, and the show was again postponed. When the show finally did air, his intro was truly memorable, as was Ellen DeGeneres's performance. She struck the perfect tone and, although I don't write for her, I did give one joke to her, which got a pretty big laugh.

She said, "I think it's important for us to be here. Because they can't take away our creativity, our striving for excellence, our joy . . . only network executives can do that."

She ad-libbed an even better line: "I feel like I'm in a unique position as host. Because, think about it: What would bug the Taliban more than seeing a gay woman in a suit surrounded by Jews?"

I had a childhood nickname. Icepick. When I was eight years old, my parents would drop me off Sunday mornings at my dad's beer distributorship at Sixtieth and Lancaster in Philadelphia. Very tough neighborhood. They'd drop me off at eight a.m. with a pocketful of quarters and leave me there till five p.m. so I could make change for people who wanted to buy blocks of ice from my dad's vending machine. One day a drunk robbed me and, being eight years old, I was a bit traumatized. When I told my parents, my dad's first question was, naturally: How much did they take?

Gee thanks, Dad; how about an "Are you okay?"

"What do I do if that happens again?" I asked. Dad said, "Run across the street to Continental Car Wash; they'll take care of you for a case of beer." So let me get this straight. Someone is trying to rob me, a fifty-pound eight-year-old, and his solution is to have me run across a traffic-filled four-lane street, weighed down with $50 worth of quarters and a case of beer to have some drunken car wash attendees protect me?

Mom had a much better solution. She said, "Just carry an ice pick." Great, I'm an eight-year-old Mafioso in training. When I told people that story, I instantly got the nickname.

I ended up doing neither. No dodging traffic like Eddie Murphy in *Bowfinger*. No stabbing someone in the knee like Sam Giancana in Chicago. Instead I learned how to talk my way out of any situation using humor. I'd make people laugh, I'd focus them on something else with comedy, I'd try and make them like what I was saying.

So thanks to the guy who robbed me that day; I ended up being a comedy writer.

PROLOGUE

September 29, 2014. I'm driving on the 101 in LA. Phone rings. It's Secretary of State John Kerry's office, asking if I can help with some remarks he has to give. The prime minister of India is coming to a luncheon in an hour and the secretary would like a little help with what he is going to say. He needs a light ice-breaker for the audience. I'm not good coming up with jokes on the phone, I need to write them out. I'm about to tell everyone at Foggy Bottom they need to wait until I pull over, when I get an incoming call. I see it is the Muppets wanting copy for Miss Piggy's duet with Michael Bublé. It's the ultimate dilemma. I tell the secretary of state's office I'll get back to them, because I need to handle Miss Piggy. After all, a mere cabinet member will be out of work in two years, and Miss Piggy is forever. As I pull over to the side of the road to write the back-and-forth between Michael Bublé and Miss Piggy, I can't help but wonder: How did I get to this place in my life?

INTRODUCTION

February 6, 2014. 6:15 a.m. I got up at the usual time, looked at *Drudge* to see if there were any red flashing sirens heralding a major event. There was nothing major that morning, so I looked at the secondary stories of the day, went to the *National Journal Hotline* for political news, *Fark* for odd stories, and *TMZ* to see whose house Justin Bieber had egged. I started to make my daily list of nine stories (no real reason, just a number I came up with years ago when I started writing) that I thought were ripe for jokes for that night . . . then stopped. We were just hours away from Jay Leno's last *Tonight Show*. The monologue for that night was already pretty much locked. There was nothing to do but go in and say good-bye to people I worked with for twenty-two years.

We had a big staff, well over one hundred people—anywhere from fourteen to eighteen writers. Our writers were divided into three types: monologue writers, sketch/taped piece/bit writers, and those like me who went both ways. If you did both, your primary responsibility was the monologue, the bread and butter of the show, but we also came up with bit ideas and contributed to those that were in the works. At the heart of anything we did, whether a joke or a bit, was this: Is it funny?

Which leads to people often asking me, "How did you get to be funny?" Actually, critics ask, "Why do you have a job? You're not funny." To the former I tell this story. My dad passed away in 2013. A few months later I was over visiting my mom in her assisted-living place, and when I went into her room there was a ninety-year-old man on a walker talking to her. First thing I said was "Mom, too soon." Nothing. Crickets. When the gentleman left, I said, "Mom, you could do better, someone more mobile, have you checked if he's in the Forbes 400?" No reaction. She then said, "Oh, he was here to thank me. When your dad died, he had two boxes of Depends left over. They were sitting in the closet, and George needed them." I said, "That is so sweet." She said, "So I sold the Depends to him." That, ladies and gentlemen, is where the comedy comes from.

All the guys I grew up with were funny; as were, probably, the people you grew up with. The only difference between them and me is that I typed out the funny comments I thought of. It actually started in sixth grade. We had to write a two-page essay about our family. Everyone in Mrs. McMann's class wrote about their real family. I made up funny stories about an older brother and younger sister who didn't exist. I got an A-plus. That was the start of comedy writing. So you can either thank or blame Mrs. McMann at Woodland Avenue Junior High after you finish this book.

A lot of people are funny; so how did I end up on late night as Jonny the Joke Boy? After law school—I know, I know, we all make mistakes—I started running political campaigns. After winning my first two campaigns and being on the cover of *Philadelphia* magazine as one of eighty-one people to watch in '81 (one of the other people ended up killing a police officer, so I figure I ended up in eightieth place out of eighty-one), I proceeded to lose twenty-three straight races. If I backed the hare, the tortoise won. If I went all in on the tortoise, the hare won. Finally in 1986 a man named Bob Casey ran for governor of Pennsylvania. He had run and lost three times before and was known as the "three-time loss from Holy Cross." Not many people were rushing out to work for Casey. Meanwhile, no one would hire me, along with another guy named James Carville, who I believe had the same campaign track record as me. We teamed up with Casey, and he won his primary and general election. We were hot stuff, and my wife, Julie, and I and James moved to DC. Not into the same apartment. Get your filthy minds out of the gutter.

I moved up from local campaign hack to being a *national* political media guru at a top consulting firm named Doak, Shrum and Associates. I was half of the associates, the other being Steve McMahon. The differences between a hack and a consultant are better suits, a company credit card, and having people more likely to believe my bullshit. My friend Donna Brazile said that political consultants back then were all basically fat white guys in suits. I was not fat. We were, however, white boys in suits.

I ended up doing pretty well at national strategy, making TV ads, and handling debate prep, and got to meet some amazing people, as well as a few candidates best described as empty suits. In 1990, one of my clients, Senator Paul Simon, who was not an empty suit, was asked to do the Gridiron speech. The Gridiron, like sex after age sixty, is a much-anticipated, once-a-year event. Except this one has an audience. All the big-deal political reporters put on skits, and then a member of each party, one Democrat and one Republican, are expected to give funny speeches. Paul called me and said, "Jon, you're funny, write some jokes."

Paul thought I was funny based on the day when he and I were driving back from a speech he gave, and we passed a car with a bumper sticker that read SAVE A TREE, EAT A BEAVER. Paul suddenly said, "Why would anyone want to eat a beaver?" I did what I do best in moments like this: I pretended to be asleep for the next ten minutes, as Chuck the driver explained the difference between the beaver on the bumper sticker and the furry little creature with big teeth. Silence for the next hour of the drive, as Paul contemplated an act that had not heretofore entered his mind. At the end of the drive, as he got out of the car, he turned to us and said, "I still can't understand why anyone would eat a beaver."

Regardless, two things happened. His wife, Jeanne, looked really happy the next time I saw her, and Paul decided I was funny because I laughed at his "I still can't understand why anyone would eat a beaver" line, so he asked me to write some jokes for the Gridiron.

Here is where it gets interesting. Paul gives the speech and it *kills*. Mr. Deadpan in the Bowtie is now Shecky Greene. Frank Mankiewicz, who put together the speech, called afterward to say my jokes were great and I ought to do this for a living. At that point I figured maybe that was Frank's very nice way of saying I was a really bad political consultant.

So that was in the back of my mind in 1991 when I saw Jay Leno perform his stand-up act at Wolf Trap in Vienna, Virginia. I was completely blown away. It was the best stand-up act I ever saw. The timing, the jokes, the performance, the delivery.

And his show was timeless, there was nothing topical about it. This was before he had been named to take over *The Tonight Show* from Johnny. In the *Washington Post* the morning of Jay's performance was an article saying Jay bought jokes from free-lancers, so, what the hell, I sent in some jokes and got a freelance agreement back in the mail. *Whoa!* I figured, *I'm hot stuff. They must be having big meetings at NBC about me and my incredible talent.* Only later did I find out that I was one of nine hundred freelancers who had the standard agreement. If Jay used a joke, I'd get fifty dollars. So I sent in my first batch, and on July 11, 1991, when he was still guest-hosting for Carson, I heard him use one of my jokes.

"There was a solar eclipse today. This throws everything off when it gets dark in the middle of the day. The birds stop chirping. The cows come in from the pasture. The hookers come out on Times Square."

That was it. The worst joke ever written. And then the check came for fifty dollars. I was a professional comedy writer. I felt like the first girl off the bus from Minneapolis in LA who now gets paid for the sex act she did back home to all the guys for free. I framed the check until my wife said, "Idiot, you make a copy and frame it. Cash the actual check."

So I kept sending in jokes for the one day a week Jay would guest-host, and he would use one or two a week. Then he was officially named Johnny Carson's replacement starting the following May, and he did an entire week of shows in October while Johnny took a break. That week he used five of my jokes and sent me a bonus check.

It was fun. I'd write jokes on the plane as I would fly from state to state doing ads in US Senate and governors' races, go into the hotel, pay the desk clerk ten dollars to let me use his giant forty-foot desktop, type up the jokes I had written on the plane, print them, and fax them to Jay. Then in January 1992 we had our third kid. Not Jay and me—Julie and me. All my kids are blond, I'm dark-skinned with dark hair, and I was on the road three hundred nights a year. Go ask my wife whose they are. It's too late to get jealous.

I was in Utah on a losing US Senate race when I got a call from Helga in Jay's office. She said Jay hadn't gotten my fax that day and could I resend. I said, "I had no idea my jokes meant anything." She said, "You mean Jay hasn't called you?" Five minutes later Jay called and said, "Hey, I'm putting together my staff, would you want to be considered?" Not a job offer but a "Would you consider?"

Now, when the job offer actually came it meant giving up a big job as a partner in a top DC consulting firm, to go move across country with three little kids and start a new job in a business that has a 99 percent failure rate. I said, "Sure."

Three weeks later I was on a TV shoot for a losing candidate for Congress in Virginia (my losing streak was under way again) when my wife called the campaign headquarters. "Jay offered you the job," she said. "I told him yes."

I called Jay so that I could actually accept, but had to confess something: I had clients through November and partners, and was worried that might be a deal breaker. He said, "You can do both—fly back and forth, send in jokes, and move out to LA in November."

I'm thinking, *That's two full-time jobs.* That meant I would have to get up every morning at five, write jokes for four hours, work as a political consultant, fly to a new Senate race every other day, finish at nine at night, and then prime the pump by writing jokes for the next day. It was insane. So I said yes.

So I took the job with Jay, did two jobs for six months, moved out to Los Angeles in November 1992, told my partners this would last thirteen weeks and then I'd be back so keep the partnership open. It's now 2015. I think they've given away my office. One thing led to another. Working for Jay gave me the chance over the years to meet and begin working for other comedians. Thanks to a recommendation from my old boss Bob Shrum, Don Mischer hired me to write the Emmys in 1995, then Billy Crystal called and asked me to write the Oscars in 1997. Billy introduced me to Whoopi, who hired me to write her Oscars a year later. Billy passed my name on to Steve Martin, who hired me for when he hosted. Chris Rock called Steve a few years later and hired me on Steve's recommendation. Steve also recommended me to Marty Short. Billy and a comedy writer and close friend named Dave Boone introduced me to Hugh Jackman in 2005, and Hugh hired me to write the Tonys. So, like the town whore, I got passed around. Many of you are asking, "What's a town whore?" Usually about fifty dollars.

At this point, I've written shows, speeches, bits, monologues, and jokes for all of the above, plus Terry Fator, Eva Longoria, Felicity Huffman, Michael Bublé, Michael Douglas, Morgan Freeman, and Terry Bradshaw. Meanwhile, thanks to my political friends, as of the writing of this book, I've written for twenty senators and governors and a few US presidents and vice presidents. But those are fun things I did on the side. In the end, nothing was more important than the mother ship, *The Tonight Show with Jay Leno*.

On a typical workday at *The Tonight Show* I wrote jokes in batches of ten and brought them into Jay's office every thirty minutes or so. He would read them along with the lines from the other writers and pick ones that were possibly monologue-worthy. He read more than a thousand jokes a day, would pick a hundred or so he liked, and then he and head writer Jack

Coen would select the best twenty-five-plus for the monologue. Some were holdovers from the night before, others new from that day. Once they picked the jokes, Jay would go down to rehearse the comedy bits, then go over the monologue, put it in order, and do the show from four to five p.m. It's what we called a live taping, meaning the mistakes stay in. There'd be a retape if an aging singer forgot the words to his own song. Or if a drugged-out young singer forgot the words to hers. That's the advantage Britney Spears has—the pretaped recording never forgets.

Some writers like the TV on, have earbuds in, and are listening to Lil Wayne when they type out jokes. For me, I need a computer, a couple newspapers spread out, and total quiet. Not because I'm in that "Shh, genius at work mode." But because I'm not smart enough to do two things at once.

Every day, by late afternoon, I would have an inkling of how many jokes of mine had made it into the monologue, but I would have to watch to see if they survived whatever final preshow cut there may have been, and how they worked. Bottom line: if I got five in, it was a fantastic night; four, really good; three, solid; two made me depressed; one had me suicidal; and on the nights when I got nothing in, someone would call my wife and tell her to hide the dog and kids before I got home.

The last show was not typical. We had so many special segments planned, including a Billy Crystal song and tribute to Jay, plus Jay's farewell at the end, that the monologue was going to be short. Since I figured it would be only about ten jokes long instead of the usual number, I worried I wouldn't have even one joke on the last show. It's bad enough to not have any jokes in the monologue on any night, but at least knowing there's a show the next night can make up for it. Not having any jokes and having no other show to look forward to would be crushing. Yes, I'm that shallow, self-centered, and neurotic. Jay's last night, and somehow I decide it's about me. That explains why I'm in show business.

I'm also really superstitious. In twenty-two years I never watched the show from the floor. And it worked. By not going downstairs for the taping, I had a job in show business for more than one thousand consecutive paychecks. Instead I always watched on the TV in my office and continued to work on jokes for the next night, but like the Pesach seder, this night was different from all other nights.

I liked Jay's last monologue. It had a few jokes about the occasion and a few topical. Jay was halfway through the monologue and hadn't done any jokes of mine. I had helped Billy Crystal write his tribute to Jay (okay, I typed word for word what Billy dictated over the phone, but that's close enough to say I was part of his brilliant segment), so I knew I was contributing to the last show, but, still, I wanted at least one joke. Again Mr. Shallow. Then I heard Jay do it . . . my last joke on his show.

"Over the years people want to know if David Letterman and I dislike each other. Not true. We like each other and we've had a long relationship. We both realize no one wants to turn on TV and see millionaires fighting. That's what Republican primaries are for."

Okay, I had sent in the joke with the word *presidential* before *primaries*, and he left it out, but so be it. The joke scored and it was a political joke, one that, given my background, was right in Jay's wheelhouse and mine.

Later in the show Billy did his tribute and then ended his segment with a great song he and Marc Shaiman put together, with cameos from huge stars like Carol Burnett and Oprah and fake stars like Kim Kardashian. Jay gave a good-bye, Garth Brooks sang us off the air, and that was it.

The wrap party was nice, my wife and I mingled, then we sat with Jay and Mavis Leno and Billy and Janice Crystal until it was time to go. It was the typical crappy LA finger food, so Julie and I went to Dan Tana's, I had one martini too many, and we went home. Four thousand, six hundred ten *Tonight Shows with Jay Leno* and it was over.

I was one of eight writers on Jay's first show on May 25, 1992, and one of only two who made it with him the entire time he was the host. Let's do the math: 4,610 shows, 100-plus monologue jokes written a day, plus with what I wrote for sketches, it's about 500,000 jokes. Being a baseball numbers nerd, I kept a count, and about 18,000 of mine made it on the air. Being a bit self-loathing, I prefer to think that means 482,000 jokes are in a landfill somewhere.

Let me take a moment and note for anyone who thinks I am egotistic that I was involved in three shows that *Entertainment Weekly* and other reviewers called among *the worst of all time.*

One is the Franco-Hathaway Oscars. Not my fault, not her fault, his fault.

The Emmys hosted by the five reality-show hosts. Four Marx Brothers worked together five-plus nights a week for fourteen years and decided four people onstage was too much, so Zeppo left. Five people, no matter how talented, working together for the first time *live* are just not going to be a success.

And Jay's ten o'clock show. Let me just say it was not the best idea NBC ever had. Jay was born for late night.

I think all of us knew deep down it was doomed to fail. But we did find out later that you can un-ring a bell. We went back to where we should have stayed the entire time.

I'm proud of my time with Jay. Somebody once told me I had more jokes on television than any writer in history, but the person who told me that was my manager, David Steinberg, and I pay him. Still, it could be true. I'd like to believe it. Just as I'd like to believe my congressman when he tells me he cares about me and my family. In 2004, *Newsday* ranked me the sixth-most important player in television influencing coverage of the presidential election, right after Jon Stewart and between Tom Brokaw and Rush Limbaugh. As Marty Short would say, "Jon, it's safe to say you're really important; not true, but safe to say."

What I did isn't important like what a surgeon does, however being a late-night writer for that long was a unique position to occupy. As a monologue writer on the number-one show for two decades, I read tens of thousands of news stories. It was my decision what to write about and to give a joke the spin I thought would work. There was rarely from Jay any "Don't do this joke" or "Let's do jokes on Senator Schmuck." And when he did nix something, it was only because he had too many from all of us on the same topic. Like the jokes I always sent in when a guy fell into a wood chipper. It happens in LA every three months—a guy gets chopped to pieces, and we comedy writers think it's hysterical. Goodbye, Mr. Chips. There was no way Jay would ever do those, but we wrote them anyway. And then at some point in the day he'd say, "No more wood-chipper jokes." It's a shame, because if we had done the jokes, it would have alerted people to the dangers of wood chippers and those jokes might have saved lives. Which would have made my job as important as a surgeon's.

So we were on our own in choosing topics, and simply by virtue of that freedom comedy writers have an impact on what kind of jokes will be told. And if I'm only writing jokes about the fact that Barack Obama plays too much golf and has abdicated his job, and if all the other writers are doing the same type of jokes, then those are what Jay and his head writers over the years, Jimmy Brogan and Jack Coen, would have to pick from. Limited topics in, limited topics out. Which is why Jay always wanted and encouraged us to write about anything and everything.

Now, he's never going to do anything counterintuitive and try to sell people on something that's not true or not believable, but when it comes to politics, what we produced joke-wise is what made it on the air. And what made it on the air is what had an impact on how people view things.

Not only was my job unique, it was an odd position for me. I had to compartmentalize and often wore two hats professionally, over the years keeping a hand in the political-consulting game. So, on one hand I was a Democrat who worked on John Kerry's and Barack Obama's campaigns. On the other, I had no problem zinging Democrats when they screwed up. In fact, I always went the other way and wrote thousands more jokes about Democrats than Republicans. When it comes to politics, I am a pro–gay rights social liberal who supports Medicare and more money for education. But when it comes to jokes, I'm a writer first, Democrat 615th. I gave David Axelrod this line after the one debate in which Hillary tried to show she knew the inner workings of the White House better than Obama: "Barack Obama for president, Hillary Clinton for chief of staff." I'm also the one who wrote that if we wanted to bring down Iran with economic sanctions, we should give them Obamacare.

Back to the *Newsday* quote—which is where the idea for this book came from—does Jon Stewart or anyone in late night (including this lowly writer) really have an impact on presidential elections? Does one joke we laugh at before going to bed turn the tide of public thinking?

Are the jokes all of us have watched performed on late-night shows important? Do they matter in the larger sense? Or are all of us who write for late night just immature class clowns too unattractive to be stars in front of the camera? Is it true that as a comedy writer you can look at YouPorn on your work computer and not get in trouble because it's "research"? The answer to at least two of those questions is yes.

So that's what this book is (mostly) about. Not the unattractive-writer part, but the larger meaning of how late-night comedy monologues and sketches can influence and impact us. We watch late-night TV for a number of reasons: to forget about the troubles of the day, to avoid having sex, to have something to do after sex, or even during it. But the main reason is to watch the monologue and comedy bits. Let's be honest, does anyone really stay up until midnight to watch second guest Andrew Garfield talk about the tremendous challenge of playing Spider-Man? Do we really want to hear about how when he was a lonely ten-year-old and all the other kids made fun of him, it was Peter Parker who gave him strength to survive? *Zzzzz*. Try telling a kid growing up in Syria how tough your life is, Andrew. And that's not to single out Andrew Garfield, I think he is a wonderful actor. But does anyone stay up until 12:29 to see some third-rate indie band sing a song that sounds like a song by a third-rate indie band? The drop-off in the number of viewers who stop watching after the monologue and first comedy bit on a late-night show is anywhere from 20 to 30 percent. We stay up for the monologue because it puts things in perspective; then a lot of us go to sleep. No matter how good or shitty a day it's been, we all feel better and sleep easier being able to laugh at the fact that the emperor has no clothes, that the politicians and celebrities we see on TV or the big screen are just as flawed as the rest of us.

Moreover, and that's a word I like to use because they told us in law school it sounds really impressive and you can bill clients more that way, what we see on late night gives us topics to talk about the next day. It used to be called "watercooler" conversation back in the old days. People would gather around the watercooler in the office and talk about what Johnny had said the night before. In the digital age, you get someone forwarding you a clip of what Stewart did the night before, or a text, "Did you see Morgan Freeman inhaling helium on Fallon?" You look at the clip and forward it along to ten other friends. So our back-and-forth conversation still centers on what the late-night hosts are talking about or showing, and the end result is no work *ever* gets done. It's why the Chinese are outworking us and why for the first time their economy is number one. They don't have late-night TV. If we want to surpass them, we should make sure Jimmy Fallon's show is broadcast in Beijing. In fact, these clips and online conversations about late night are such important parts of our lives that sometimes we stop our shopping on Amazon at work, or playing Halo, or looking at porn. We text and e-mail and forward clips and use what the late-night shows talk about to frame our interactions. I call it the *Jersey Shore/Real Housewives of New Jersey* syndrome. Watching idiots is a way for us to say things may be bad but at least we're not *that*. Or maybe we just like laughing at New Jersey.

What do late-night shows explain about us as Americans?

How does the monologue change and shape our opinions? What do we laugh at? What can we laugh at in these overly sensitive, politically correct, it's-just-a-joke-people times? Why do jokes that work when the character Stephen Colbert plays does them live cause problems when he tries them on Twitter: i.e., his "Ching-Chong Ding-Dong Foundation for Sensitivity to Orientals or Whatever." In other words, why do jokes matter so much, and are they a thermometer taking a temperature of and just reflecting what's out there or are they a thermostat changing "what is out there"?

Caveat one: I get the fact that jokes are not curing cancer. Then again, neither are any cancer doctors.

Caveat two: A confession. I entered politics because I wanted to change the world. After fifteen years I decided to become a comedy writer. Totally different from politics, because some comedy writers are honest and don't sleep with interns.

Another difference: Comedy writers don't try to change the world; we like it right where it is on any given day, a big fat sitting target. And although we don't change the world, we do change the way people see the world and the people and events that are in the news. If you don't believe me, ask Sarah Palin how she feels about Tina Fey.

CHAPTER ONE

King Johnny and the Princes

Although my experience has been primarily with Jay, this is about all the great late-night and sketch shows. Johnny, Jay, Dave, Jimmy Fallon, Arsenio, Jon Stewart, Stephen Colbert, *SNL*, Bill Maher, Jimmy Kimmel, and Conan—these are the shows and people who I believe have truly helped shape the way America looks at politicians, celebrities, and events.

September 27, 1954, late-night TV was born with host Steve Allen. Two interesting facts: First, *The Tonight Show* was created by Pat Weaver, Sigourney Weaver's father, and second, no one remembers Steve Allen. But they should. He invented the modern talk show format, which, like the horseshoe crab and English anti-Semitism, has remained basically unchanged for eons. If you take a horseshoe crab from today (and they are delicious in a puff pastry) and one from 400 million years ago, they look similar. There are, however, differences in late-night style, for my belief is that each host takes what others have done, builds on it, and gives it a unique twist.

Steve's show in a nutshell: Steve had an opening, music, celebrity interviews, an audience bit, and, I usually hate this word but it is perfect applied to him, a sensibility best described as zany. He also did something that is key to the success of a show—he loved to laugh, and when he cracked up in the middle of a sketch with Don Knotts or Tom Poston or Louis Nye, it signaled to the audience at home that it was time to laugh. Take a look at the old clips or at PBS's great documentary in the *Pioneers of Television* series. You can trace a line directly from Steve Allen to David Letterman.

Steve Allen left as host in early 1957 and NBC decided to tinker with a winning format. Sound familiar? This next version of *The Tonight Show* was made more like the *Today* show, with news and features. The host was the immortal Jazzbo Collins, and it ended up being, what's the word I'm looking for . . . a disaster. NBC realized its mistake and switched back to the late-night format that had worked.

Next came Jack Paar. Jack was urbane and erudite, and you got the feeling that he was a genuinely witty man. What marked Jack's reign at the top was the intellectual quality of the guests. Paar had on guests such as William F. Buckley and Peter Ustinov (Google them), and he reveled in their stories. Jack wasn't as good a joke teller as he was a storyteller. He also was willing to go where no talk-show host had gone before, doing a show in the shadow of the Berlin Wall, and interviewing Fidel Castro as well as presidential candidates John F. Kennedy and Richard Nixon. He also was the first to show the true power of television, in essence destroying the career of newspaper columnist Walter Winchell. Winchell was an ink-stained bully who went unchallenged whenever he took on those he didn't like. But Jack Paar answered back in his nightly monologues, skewering Winchell. According to Neal Gabler's book about Winchell, it began when Winchell refused to retract an item in his column saying that Paar had marriage problems. Jack used his show to claim Winchell's column was "written by a fly," that "his voice was too high because he wore too tight underwear," and that Winchell had a "hole in his soul" and was a "silly old man." Paper may beat rock, but newspapers don't beat TV. In the end, television 1, newspapers 0. Winchell's may have been the first, but his was certainly not the last career brought down by a late-night monologue.

The problem with fully describing the styles of Steve Allen and Jack Paar is like describing eight-track tapes to people younger than thirty. The fact is, Steve's and Jack's time was before my time, I didn't see them live, and very few tapes of their entire shows exist. I know Ty Cobb was a great ballplayer but I have to take the word of those who wrote about him at the time he played. These shows are like dinosaur fossils. We know dinosaurs existed, we know they were big and important, but we can't really be sure what they looked like. That is unless you're a creationist who believes that the dinosaurs were around a few thousand years ago and that they lived on a diet of ferns and very slow senior citizens. Which reminds me of a great Lewis Black joke: If you believe that dinosaurs and people lived at the same time, you think *The Flintstones* cartoon is a documentary.

So despite *The Tonight Show*'s having marked sixty years on the air, those earlier years and hosts are too far back in the historical record for me to really comment on. For our purposes, history began in October 1962, when Johnny Carson began his ninety-minute show in New York. Ninety minutes!

And what a first show. Johnny was introduced by Groucho Marx, and guests included Joan Crawford, Tony Bennett, Mel Brooks, Ed Metzger, and Rudy Vallee. Referring to his entrance as he walked onstage, his first joke was "Boy, you would think it was Vice President Nixon."

Right then and there, commenting on people who were in the news, Johnny set the tone for what was to be.

Johnny Carson was the king. Starting out in a world of three networks and not many entertainment choices, Johnny established once and for all what late-night monologues were supposed to do. People watched the evening news at dinnertime, and prime-time TV afterward—usually shows about genies, hillbillies, talking cars, and passengers stranded after a three-hour tour. He was the one who made everyone laugh at the news of the day. It was real-time viewing: no *Hulu*, no taping to watch later. You turned on the TV at eleven thirty, watched and laughed, had sex, and went to sleep. Or if you were real adventurous, you had sex while watching TV. By the way, I've tried that—the problem is, who has the remote?

Johnny took what Paar did and added great comedic bits plus something else; he made the guests funny in his interaction with them. His jokes were brilliant, and he was the one who made the monologue important by putting the focus on pop culture.

How does he rank? Ted Williams was the best hitter who ever lived, Jim Brown was the greatest running back, Ron Jeremy is the greatest porn star, and Johnny Carson is considered the best late-night host. How do we know this?

Let me make an analogy. If ten people tell you that you have a piece of spinach stuck in your teeth, you have a piece of spin-ach stuck in your teeth. When every host who came after Johnny idolizes him, when every observer of late night heaps praise on the same person and says he's the best, then guess what—he is the best.

And twenty-three years after he went off the air, Johnny Carson is still ranked number one in terms of popularity. In a 2014 survey by the people at YouGov research, 32 percent of Americans said Johnny was their favorite talk-show host of all time. Jay was second, at 8 percent, and everyone else was at 6 percent or lower.

One reason for Johnny's popularity is that he was able to use his "desk" and his interviewing style to amplify the comic brilliance of his guests. Look at any YouTube video of Carson with Don Rickles. Johnny was content knowing he was the star, and he could afford to turn the spotlight on his guests and let them shine.

I think the great Billy Wilder said it best about Johnny:

He enchants the invalids and the insomniacs as well as the people who have to get up at dawn. He is the Valium and the Nembutal of a nation. No matter what kind of dead-asses are on the show, he has to make them funny and exciting. He has to be their nurse and their surgeon. He has no conceit. He does his work and he comes prepared. If he's talking to an author, he has read the book. Even his rehearsed routines sound improvised. He's the cream of middle-class elegance, yet he's not a mannequin. He has captivated the American bourgeoisie without ever offending the highbrows, and he has never said anything that wasn't liberal or progressive. Every night, in front of millions of people, he has to do the *salto mortale* [circus parlance for an aerial somersault performed on the tightrope]. What's more, he does it without a net. No rewrites. No retakes. The jokes must work tonight.

Ladies and gentlemen of the jury, I rest my case.

Johnny is the gold standard, and anyone who followed had an impossible standard to match. And Jay Leno came as close to it as anyone could.

Caveat three: I love Jay. He is the best monologuist who ever lived, a great human being, and he made me part of the family for twenty-two years. He came to all three of my kids' bar mitzvahs, staying for the service and the reception when even I didn't want to be there; took care of an air ambulance to fly my wife home to LA after she had a stroke in Las Vegas; gave huge annual bonuses out of his own pocket to everyone on the show for twenty-two years; and made sure everyone got six months' pay when the show ended to make sure people didn't lose their houses or have to change their lifestyles. So anyone who says I'm biased in supporting him, they're fucking right. I am. It takes nothing away from Dave or anyone else to say Jay was the perfect and only person to follow Johnny. Or to say that he is the second carving on the Mount Rushmore of late-night hosts, right next to President Carson.

I'll let Bill Maher put Jay in perspective with the remarks he gave when inducting Jay into the Television Academy Hall of Fame.

Bill called Jay's twenty-two years as host "a drive down a highway in some giant, gleaming, pristine luxury car with the competition far in the rearview mirror—except one time when NBC, driving some beat-up clunker, blindsided him and beat the shit out of his beautiful car."

Bill pointed out that Johnny Carson, whom he loves, was not rebellious and edgy, while Jay is tame and mild; the truth is, they both spoke for Middle America. Bill then compared Jay to Israel. He said, "Jay isn't perfect but he's held to a standard I don't think anybody in the world is expected to live up to but him."

I love Bill Maher for that. And I think he nailed it.

Jay did more *Tonight Show*s than Johnny, and he told more jokes in his monologue than anyone. And, you know something, they didn't always work. Not every joke does. It's why Carson had his joke savers. Joke savers are comments comedians make afterward that let the audience know they're aware that the joke bombed. Example: "That joke went over like Donald Sterling at the NAACP convention." But to put Jay in baseball terms, he had more at bats and more hits than anyone who ever lived, which means by definition he was going to have some outs.

Some people like boxing, some like theater. Very few like both. Some people like Jay, some like Dave. I respect both artists.

To me, David Letterman is a true descendant of Steve Allen. Zany, especially in his earlier years, and uniquely brilliant. When Letterman likes a guest—a Billy Crystal, a Marty Short—he's an incredible host and the best audience a comic could want. The problem is that Dave can come off as cranky, and in later years has had a tendency to make it clear to the audience that he's not thrilled with a crappy guest. Johnny seemingly never did that. Johnny would fight to make a guest shine even if nothing was there. Jay had the confidence that even if he had a bad guest, he had already won, because night after night he delivered the best monologue.

Dave is a different joke teller than Jay. With Jay, you listen to the joke, react, and laugh. With Dave, you are often watching him to see how he reacts to the telling of it.

This is a perfect example of a joke where you can picture

Dave and know his attitude at that moment: "Are you excited about the new Spider-Man movie? . . . Then you're twelve."

And, please, Spider-Man fans, don't write me to say I'm picking on that franchise. As if Spider-Man fans can write.

Dave's style raises the question of whether we like to feel uncomfortable watching an uncomfortable host. Dave clearly is not happy in his own skin, and there's a sense of danger around him. Johnny wasn't dangerous, nor was Jay. Dave is dangerous, and I mean that in good way. That personality edge is appealing to a lot of people, they love the mischievous part of Dave, the unpredictability, but in the end the reason Jay was number one in the ratings for nineteen years was because Americans don't like "uncomfortable" and unpredictable late at night as much as critics do. It's also maybe why Jimmy Fallon dominates the ratings now. He's just more fun and easier to watch than anyone else on late night.

Conan O'Brien is a truly brilliant writer, and as a host he can be criticized for nothing greater than the fact that for some people he is hard to watch on stage. He has been on the air for twenty-two years but still has some of the same nervous mannerisms he had in 1993. They're real and not forced . . . which in many ways is the key to his success. Conan has never come off slick; he has always been real and that "going against the grain" is why his fans and supporters are so passionate.

Jimmy Fallon is the perfect host for a new generation of TV viewers. Young and young looking, he is likable in the Leno vein and innovative in a way that connects with younger viewers. He has the willingness to try new things as Conan did in the nineties and has the format in which they can be seen. Jimmy is an excellent impersonator and musician, is non-threatening (like Johnny and Jay), and is polite to his guests (like Johnny and Jay), which means that celebrities are willing to go along with what he suggests. And that can result in comedy gold. This may not always go over well with older celebrities like Don Rickles, who, when asked if he was going on Jimmy's show, kiddingly said, "I don't play Ping-Pong." But that's not who Jimmy is after. He's not going for retro hip, he's aiming at young and current hip, and can get a president to slow-jam the news, Emma Stone to lip sync, or have Marty Short and Jerry Seinfeld play Pictionary. Jimmy has taken late night to a new and next level. He owns it, it's his show and he clearly loves what he's doing. He is having so much fun that we have fun just watching him. My prediction: he will be the king (or at least the top prince) for the next twenty years.

Another difference between Jimmy and other hosts is that Jimmy spends less time talking to guests and more time on comedy bits and music. According to communications experts at Grand View University (which is a real college, even though it sounds made up; it's in Iowa and the mascot is the fighting boll weevil—okay, I made the last part up), Johnny, Dave, Jay, and Seth Meyers all spent 51 percent of their shows talking while Jimmy spends 37 percent. And Jimmy spends 23 percent of his time on comedy and 14 percent on music, a much higher percentage than Jay and Johnny allowed. Jimmy has made his show successful by making it more of a variety show than what in England would be called a chat show.

Jon Stewart has created his own unique late-night show that is influential, smart, and funny. Jon makes his point with commentary and comic acting. For a long time I didn't realize that he is in fact an incredibly strong stand-up and joke teller. I knew he had done stand-up and heard he was good, but it never clicked until I watched Jon at the Don Rickles birthday salute. He *killed*. The salute was called *One Night Only: An All-Star Tribute to Don Rickles*. Jon started with "One night only, that's all the doctor said, huh? I'll keep my remarks brief." He pointed to the table where Don was seated with Robert De Niro, Martin Scorsese, Regis Philbin, Johnny Depp, and Jerry Seinfeld and said, "Nice wingmen, by the way. You're really getting laid tonight."

A total pro as a stand-up. But that's not where Jon makes his money. He makes it with his show and attitude and ability to invite us into his point of view. He has been incredibly influential in the world of politics and his recent decision to end his time on *The Daily Show* is yet another major game changer. For all fans of late night and smart political comedy he will be missed.

To give you an idea of how good he is, NBC explored having Jon host *Meet the Press*. Then, at the end of 2014, *Meet the Press* devoted a segment to whether Jon Stewart is bad for America. GMAFB (Give me a fucking break). The roundtable talked about whether Jon's show is too snarky or whether it inspires cynicism. My answer: Whorish, moneygrubbing congressmen who lie, cheat, steal, and vote to preserve their jobs rather than spend their time as public servants are why we are cynical. If anything, Jon shining the bright hot light of his show on Washington's hypocrisy and failures is what keeps us from becoming more cynical. He gives us hope that when things are wrong they can be "righted." We need Jon there every night to rip apart the Dick Cheneys of the world who think that torture is the American Way.

Bill Maher is one of my favorites, and not just for his pro-Leno comments. Like Jon Stewart, he's smart, funny, and opinionated and is a great joke teller. I'd rank him second only to Leno in the latter. His only weakness (or maybe it's his strength) is that he sometimes seems willing to take the joke a notch too far, not for the laugh but to make the point that he's willing to cross the line. Once in a while I get the feeling that it's edge for the sake of edge. Having said that, I would add that there is an audience for his brand of comedy, and HBO is the perfect home for him. What I also like about Bill is that he listens to his guests; sure, he has a point he wants to make, but he does it in context and he reacts to what they are saying. Some hosts have a tendency to say what they want, regardless of the context. Not Maher; his approach is all about flow, and for me, it's a must-watch.

And Bill is powerful enough to start a national dialogue. When you have the Sunday-morning shows and the cable news shows talking about what you said, you are a trendsetter, not a trend follower. On a show in October 2014, he called out Islam for the violence of some of its adherents, then a few days later he doubled down, when he condemned liberals for being too afraid to denounce violence committed in Islam's name. That started a back-and-forth of criticism and support of Bill; regardless of your feelings about Islam, he has the guts to raise issues that need to be addressed.

If you watch Bill and Jon and John Oliver you have a range of edgy-smart to likable-smart. Think of Leno and Johnny and Dave as three men who told the jokes and let them stand on their own; if they were making a point, it was hidden in the joke. Jon and Bill and John are more like prosecutors. They lay out the case, and Jon uses his clips and acting and personality to "convict" the guilty, Bill uses his sharp edge, and John Oliver uses his outrage.

Stephen Colbert belongs in a special category. He's not a joke teller, he's an actor playing a character, and what's amazing is that he never breaks that character. A truly extraordinary and disciplined comic. It's going to be fascinating to see what he brings to CBS when he takes over for Letterman. Somewhere there's a joke for Stephen about how CBS stands for Colbert Broadcasting System. That joke is my gift to him. Don't even need to send the fifty-dollar freelance fee.

Jimmy Kimmel, like Jimmy Fallon, has a lot of success getting celebrities to "play along" with him. Where he scores with viewers time and time again are his bits like "I'm Fucking Ben Affleck" and in the good rapport he has with comedic guests like Billy Crystal and Marty Short.

Arsenio. Let's not talk about Arsenio 2.0, which was like watching Kobe Bryant try to play in 2014. All the instincts were still there, all the things we liked about him were still there, but it just wasn't the same. It was as if Arsenio had been frozen in 1994 and thawed out, but no one told him it was 2014. I admire him for trying, and in truth, I wish he had never gone off the air in 1994. He was hip before Jimmy Fallon and he had guts—remember his post–LA riots interview. But the world changed and Arsenio had not. I recall watching Arsenio in the old days, and Warren Beatty was on to promote *Dick Tracy*. Arsenio asked him what it was like to sleep with Madonna, and Warren said, "I don't know, what's it like sleeping with Eddie Murphy?" That to me is where Arsenio was in 2014, still trapped in that Eddie Murphy era.

As I'm writing this—well, not exactly right now, but in the past few weeks—CBS named James Corden to follow Colbert and take over Craig Ferguson's old spot. I didn't know much about James other than he was a Tony Award winner, but then I got a chance to meet him. We had a great talk for about an hour about late night, and he totally gets it. At the time of this writing, his show has not yet debuted, but after watching him in *Gavin & Stacey*, I can see why CBS chose him. An awesome talent.

Now, what about the women of late night? Well, now that Chelsea Handler is off the air for a while there's . . . Wait, how can there be no women? I loved Chelsea's show and I'm thrilled she is working on a new show for Netflix. She is funny, has brass ovaries, and is a good joke teller. I really thought she might get Letterman's spot, but it went to Colbert. I actually predicted it. I'm usually right in my predictions about 10 percent of the time, which puts me 70 percent behind most of this book's readers and 9 percent ahead of the average TV executive.

Bottom line: It seems absurd to me that with all the late-night shows and slots Chelsea is the only one in the past few years to have gotten a chance. It seems that some network or cable channel would take a great female comic and give her a shot.

So in addition to Chelsea, which other women should have one? How about Amy Poehler or Amy Schumer? Hey, if there can be two Jimmys, why not two Amys? Either Amy or both would be a great addition to late night. I loved Wanda Sykes's show when it was on; let's give her another shot. And when I'm asked to run a network, I will give them all a show.

I've come up with a pretty good way to categorize the hosts. And it's based on my theory that all of life is just high school on a larger scale and without a curfew. Each host—or at least most of them—is just a grown-up version of people we met in high school.

JOHNNY CARSON—the coolest kid around, captain of the football team

JAY LENO—the funniest guy in the class, well liked, never mean

DAVID LETTERMAN—the sarcastic teacher who everyone wanted for at least one year because he was really funny

BILL MAHER—the wiseass who got suspended

JIMMY FALLON—the class clown, the one who made everyone laugh by being willing to do anything

JIMMY KIMMEL—the senior who was funny, sarcastic, and a little mean to the underclassmen

JON STEWART AND CONAN O'BRIEN—the smartest kids in class who got into Harvard and no one minded, even if they had to go to Boston College

CRAIG FERGUSON AND JOHN OLIVER—the foreign exchange students, the ones who knew how to get weed, not the girl from Trinidad who put out

STEPHEN COLBERT—the star of the drama department

CHAPTER TWO

What Makes a Great Late-Night Host

There are five elements that go into making a great late-night host. Just like there are five "tools" in making a great baseball player (hitting for average, power, fielding, throwing, speed). The elements for a host are monologue delivery; rapport with guests; willingness to ask the question or make the comment that is on everyone's mind; likability; the ability to feed the monster and constantly come up with new lines and bits over a sustained period.

Carson had all five; Jay had all five. But there are gradations. Jay had a better monologue, Johnny had a better back-and-forth with guests. But the latter has a lot to do with the era in which they were hosts. During Johnny's day, guests came on the show and stayed. They would move down the couch so that by the end of the show you would see Johnny talking to Bob Hope while Dean Martin and George Gobel joined in, cut up, and made it a free-for-all. It was a great tennis match between people who all knew each other. Johnny could rely less on his monologue and bits because the guests were willing to do more. That may be changing back, thanks to the two Jimmys, who really engage their guests with bits and taped pieces. During my time with *The Tonight Show*, one rarely got the feeling that we got during the Carson years, that the stars would really hang out together and go to dinner at Chasen's. They didn't know each other and couldn't fake it like the old-timers did. A star would show up, plug his movie, and leave to do the premiere. That left much greater pressure on the monologue to entertain. Side note—I did get to go to Chasen's once after a show when James Carville and Bob Woodward were on. I felt "old school"; I'm just surprised Woodward didn't write a book about it.

The other difference is that in the "old days," stars would come on just to be guests, with nothing to plug. You would see a John Lennon come on Dick Cavett or a Bob Newhart come on Johnny just to talk. That is rare nowadays, with only the real comedic geniuses willing to do that.

Now let's take Jimmy Fallon to see where he stands in the "five tools": likability, check; ability to come up with great new material, check; rapport with guests, check; monologue, getting there, but in the way he has transformed late night, a Leno-like monologue isn't needed on his show; willingness to make a point with a question or comment—95 percent there. Jimmy is great and getting better by the day; he has truly given new life to late night.

I think Jay's strength is that he is a legendary comic who evolved into a host willing to ask the questions and make a comment, whether to a Hugh Grant or to an elected official stopping by the show. The difference I guess between the two is that politicians rarely pay for sex.

So what made Jay such a great host? By the time he took over *The Tonight Show*, he had years of experience speaking in front of every kind of audience—corporate, nightclub, comedy club—and was used to things going wrong in a live setting. He could instantly handle the lights going out, a heckler, a drunk. He wasn't a singer or someone trapped by a taped show—he was a live, in-the-moment, on-the-stage comic. It's why the best guests tend to be comics or theater people. Film actors can be boring guests. They are used to being someone else, not themselves, and as a result, on a talk show they can be a little withdrawn. Comics have the advantage of having created a stage personality they can rely on, and theater stars are used to appearing live.

Another plus Jay has is that as an Everyman who sees himself as no one's superior and as no one's supplicant, he has never been intimidated by "important" people. He represented our voice, he spoke for the audience, and like Oprah in daytime he asked the questions we wanted to ask and said what we would say.

What also made him successful was that he always knew exactly who he was and never lost his brand. He didn't try to be a serious interviewer, he never emulated Dick Cavett—it wasn't his thing, and wasn't believable.

Jay's success reminds me of a story about George W. Bush. He was having lunch with a good friend of mine in 1999 and talking about running for president. He said, "I don't know if I'll run, but if I do, I'll win." My friend, who is a Democrat, thought it was the usual political bragging and said, "Why do you say that? Every candidate says that." W turned to him and said, "Because I know exactly who I am and Al Gore has no idea who he is." You know something? W nailed it.

Jay knows exactly who he is. He is the same onstage, in the office, and when he stops on the 101 to help a motorist in a broken-down 2002 Nissan Sentra change a flat tire. To me, Johnny knew exactly who people *wanted* him to be. There's a difference. Johnny maintained that brand even though that may not have been who he really was. Jay also kept his brand because his brand was him. In the end, what made him a great host is that he is a comic who knows how to make people laugh.

There is one other ingredient to Leno's success that can't be overlooked: his work ethic. The job is a lot more than the one hour a night people see you on TV. Jay would get in at eight a.m., start working on jokes, meet with producers, talk about guests, rehearse, go to the cue cards and do a read-through, do the show, and then go out and shoot a tape for a bit that would air later that week. He'd then get home and start reviewing jokes for the next day and talk with Jack Coen about the next day's monologue. Five nights a week, forty-seven weeks a year . . . plus on Sunday he would work on Monday's show.

So that's what made Jay a great host—he kept his brand, he was funny, and he outworked everybody. That's how you end up being only the seventeenth recipient of the Kennedy Center Mark Twain Prize for Humor, joining legends such as Richard Pryor, Billy Crystal, Steve Martin, Bob Newhart, and Carol Burnett.

I helped write that show in October 2014. Jerry Seinfeld killed, Wanda Sykes was amazing, and I got to work with Garth Brooks. Now, I'm a huge country fan and a huge Garth fan, so when the call came that he was doing the show, I got really fired up. Then they told me he didn't want to sing but that he wanted to tell jokes. This is a little like having Scarlett Johansson wear a burqa, but so be it. My initial thought was, *This could be a problem.* Telling jokes is hard enough for a comic. Garth is funny, but he is a singer in a room that wanted great comedy. So the solution I came up with was to have him tell fake bad roast jokes. With a drummer giving rim shots. To try to craft great jokes and count on his delivery wouldn't work. But by putting it in roast format, and putting the onus on the rim shot, I felt it would work. And it did.

Two sample jokes: "Success didn't give Jay a swelled head. Nature did that." Rim shot.

"I don't feel sorry for Jay for having such a big head. I feel sorry for the people sitting behind Jay." Rim shot.

When we were doing the BET Awards, Chris Rock, who is as funny and brilliant in everyday conversation as he is onstage, told me that some comics have jokes and others don't. If you don't, you're not going to last. And the difference between a great comic and a bad one is that they often have the same jokes in front of them before they go onstage, but the bad comic picks the wrong jokes. It's a lot like politicians during a primary campaign. Six candidates run for the same Senate seat in a primary, and they all know what the issues are, but the bad candidates pick the wrong one.

So talent is really choice. In terms of late night, the funniest comic is Leno, and after him I'd go with Maher and Fey. The most interesting late-night performers (going beyond just jokes) were Letterman and Carson, with Fallon quickly moving up there. The funniest people in the world who make me laugh are, once again, in alphabetical order, Billy Crystal, Jay Leno, Steve Martin, Chris Rock, and Martin Short.

But, Jon, this book is supposed to be about late-night comedy, why veer off? For two reasons. First, I am contractually bound to write a certain number of words, and, two, because to have an impact, you have to be funny. And to me that means saying something that people repeat days, weeks, and years later. If you can do that, you have influenced pop culture.

Look at Chris Rock at the BET Awards. Brilliant. He "defended" Donald Sterling. Check out Rock's performance on YouTube. His eight minutes are as good as any I've ever seen.

At award shows, there are hosts who do jokes "for the room," and there are hosts who care only about the audience watching at home and ignore the room, and then there are the masters who can do both. Billy Crystal is the master. The nine times he hosted the Academy Awards he did both. The difference between big award shows and late night is that in late night you are doing untried jokes that reach four million people. And if you have an off night, you have the next night to recover. It's like being a baseball player. If you go 0 for 4 on Friday but 2 for 4 Saturday and Sunday, you're .333. Keep that up over fifteen years and you are in the hall of fame. The Oscars and Golden Globes (which I've also been lucky enough to write for) are more like the Super Bowl. You have one shot with untried jokes in front of tens of millions of people watching at home and an uptight industry crowd in front of you. And there's no game the next week. Hosting late night is hard. Hosting the Golden Globes and Oscars may be the one show-business job that's harder.

I've written for eighteen Academy Award shows. I think I am fourth all-time, with no chance of ever catching up with Hal Kanter, Buz Kohan, and Bruce Vilanch. I am honored to be a distant fourth. At the Oscars and Golden Globes, there are writers who write the show and those who write for the host. Often at the Oscars there is a head writer for each set of writers—head writer is my favorite title, because it sounds just dirty enough. I've been both, and some years, for Steve Martin and Hugh Jackman, I've been in charge of both staffs. The Oscars is the show that people have asked me about the most, although as of late, the Golden Globes has caught up, thanks to the amazing work of Ricky Gervais as host and then Tina and Amy.

One of the best experiences I ever had on the Oscars was

working with Billy when he put together those openings in which he appeared in the scenes of the best films. Everyone does that now, but it was Billy who owns it. He changed the Oscars forever.

I have one great censor story from the Oscars. In 1997, Billy was the host and he was doing his popular song medley about the nominated movies. The special-material song we had come up with for *The English Patient* was to do our own lyrics to "Wouldn't It Be Loverly" from *My Fair Lady*. In one of the lines we used the word *schmuck*, and this got ABC Standards and Practices guru Susan Futterman upset. She said we couldn't use the word *schmuck*. We agreed and put the word *cluck* in the prompter and in the script; everyone was happy, even though the word made no sense, and Billy went out, killed in the opening, and then said "schmuck." The nation did not crumble, and life went on.

Another memorable time at the Oscars was with Steve Martin in 2003. We were backstage, coming up to the award that Michael Moore was likely going to win. In every acceptance speech he made, at each stop along the award show circuit (a season beginning November 14 with the Hollywood Film Awards and continuing until the next November 13, when it ends with the Country Music Awards), he blasted President Bush. I was watching backstage with Steve and Dave Barry,

Bruce Vilanch, and the other writers, when they announced Moore's name. I said, "Let's get ready." Moore got on his platform and started ripping W. To the point that even Bush haters (aka Hollywood) were going, "Too much." Booing was heard.

Moore said, "We live in the time where we have fictitious election results that elect a fictitious president. We live in a time where we have a man sending us to war for fictitious reasons. Whether it's the fiction of duct tape or fiction of orange alerts, we are against this war, Mr. Bush. Shame on you. Mr. Bush, shame on you. And anytime you got the Pope and the Dixie Chicks against you, your time is up." Of course we all know Michael Moore was right, because the war ended and John Kerry was elected president.

In the forty-five seconds before Steve went out onstage we collectively came up with this joke:

"It was so sweet backstage, you should have seen it: the Teamsters were helping Michael Moore into the trunk of his limo."

To his credit, the next year Michael Moore appeared in Billy's opening film, in which he allowed us to squash him with a giant *Lord of the Rings* elephant.

Jay never did the Oscars but if he had, he would have been in the joke-oriented, Carson-Hope-Rock-Martin mold of host, unlike the Billy Crystal–Hugh Jackman–Neil Patrick Harris style of total entertainment.

One of the most interesting things that happened post–*Tonight Show* was going to Israel with Jay. I was down in New Orleans with Chris Rock when he was doing a charity event for Brad Pitt and his Make It Right foundation. By the way, just an amazing organization that builds houses for people in New Orleans's Lower Ninth Ward and elsewhere across the country. I finish helping Chris, I'm in bed, and at one a.m. the phone rings. It's Jay.

"Hey, Jon, I have to go to Israel to emcee an event for the Genesis Prize Foundation. Can you go over and check things out and get everything ready for when I get there?"

A free trip to Israel. Plus pay! Then he said, "Stay afterward for a week, and see the country, bring your wife." For some guys that would be a deal breaker, but I actually like my wife. So we went.

I got there in advance and checked out the venue. It was at the Jerusalem Theater and it was a bit different from American award shows. For one thing, they wanted Jay to enter and do his monologue with a full orchestra behind him. No comic wants to stand onstage while seventy stone-faced people with violins stare at his back where the audience can see them.

I asked if they could lower the curtain, but the director, Tevye, said no. I asked if the play-off music could be a little more upbeat, as it sounded like the theme from *Schindler's List*. I was told no. Another thing that was different is that the teleprompter reads right to left. At least for the jokes in Hebrew.

During rehearsal Jay approached the director and asked, "Do you want me to walk out?" Tevye said, "Don't walk out." So Jay stayed still and then the director started frantically waving him onstage. Jay said, "Do you want me to walk out?" Tevye again said no, Jay stood still, and the director started frantically waving again. After five minutes of "Who's on First?" we figured out that in Israel you don't "walk out onstage," you walk "in." They thought Jay was going to literally "walk out." So it's not just their writing that's backward.

During the show I got the chance to see Jay at his ad-lib best. The prime minister of Israel was at the event, and when he was onstage he went off script and kept calling for Jay to come out. During Jay's next scheduled appearance Jay said, "So, Mr. Prime Minister, this is why we have rehearsal."

Another great post–*Tonight Show* trip was in November 2014. I was writing for the American Music Awards and Pitbull was the host. So that we could spend time working on his opening he had me meet him at Kimmel, then we flew private to Miami overnight with his band and worked on the plane. Not only did we manage to write his opening on the plane with music playing, I got to become friends with a guy who is a truly amazing talent. Pitbull is smart, insightful, personable, funny, and has become one of my favorite people to work with. I told him when we first met that this would be the greatest Jewish-Cuban joint project since Hyman Roth met with Batista. Plus it looks great on the résumé to see I've worked with everyone from Pitbull to a president.

CHAPTER THREE

What Do
We Laugh At?

The bean counters at the Center for Media and Public Affairs report that, during his twenty-two-year run, Jay did more than 43,000 jokes on public figures. That seems low to me, but if we accept their count as semi-accurate, that's nine a night on people in the news.

And who is deemed monologue-worthy? Bob Smith, a great writer for Johnny Carson who also wrote for Jay, told me that, over the decades, the types of people and entities in the news who make the monologue have remained the same. There's always been the female celebrity who's a mess, the bad-boy athlete, the bad actor, the moron in the news, the befuddled Royal

Family member, the incompetent business executive, the tin-pot dictator, the clueless southerner, and the cheating male politician—why is it the pols always discover they want to spend more time with their families after they've been caught with their pants around their ankles?

Let's take the female celebrity who's a mess: Martha Raye (pause, put down the book, and Google her) became Shannen Doherty (pause, put down the book, and Google her) became Paris Hilton (any day now you will have to pause, put down the book, and Google her) became Lindsay Lohan became Miley Cyrus. When Lindsay Lohan came on *The Tonight Show*, Jay wasn't mean to her because it was so clear to everyone she was just a mess. It would have been easy to ridicule her rambling answers or to lecture her. That's not who Jay is. It also shows the difference between Jay and other hosts. Jay liked to break balls, but only with those who could take it. There's no mean streak in him that you sometimes would see emerge in other hosts. One example is with Britney Spears. She did some crazy things—the Vegas marriage, the kids with K-Fed. But when she shaved her head and went nuts and was clearly having psychiatric problems, Jay wouldn't do a joke about her. Just as no one would do a joke right now about Amanda Bynes. Of course now that Britney is better and working and making $30 million a year, things might go back to where they were if she does stupid things. And the latter is what I think is the key to comedy—trying not to make fun of what people in the news are, but of what they do.

After all, we as a nation always want someone to point out that the emperor has no clothes. Or in Britney's case, the empress has clothes, just no underclothes.

Here are the other topics Americans like to laugh at:

The weather

Bad sports teams (when in doubt, remember, the
    Cubs always stink)

Drunken airline pilots

Cruise ships adrift with raw sewage on the deck
    (that's why it's called the poop deck . . . sorry, it's
    obvious, I know, but when you write a hundred
    jokes a day, you sometimes have to pad to fill
    out a page)

The French

The economy

Hypocritical men of the cloth (yes, I mean you,
    meth-using, male-escort-fucking Ted Haggard)

Government incompetence

Horrible movies

Banks

Lawyers

Bad chain restaurants (Sizzler became the Olive
Garden)

Fast-food restaurants

Really old people

Big cities (jokes work about New York, LA, and
Chicago, but there is nothing funny about
Atlanta)

Certain states (Kentucky, Florida, Texas, West
Virginia)

People who seem like cartoon villains (*see* Dick
Cheney and Donald Trump)

Oddball stories (for example, people who have sex
with sheep, trees, picnic tables, and cars)

By the way, over the years I have written jokes about people who have had sex with all those objects. A few years ago there was a man in Washington State who had sex with more than a thousand cars. Some of the jokes were:

Even worse, it was a foreign car.

I love my cars, too, but it's more platonic.

The worst part, he was cheating on his boat.

It was a Hummer.

Police wrote it up as a rear-ending.

Okay, they're not Noël Coward, but then again, neither is Noël anymore. (Anyone younger than ninety, please Google.)

Not all of these topics or people we deem monologue-worthy fit under one umbrella, but if there is a common link, it's that we as Americans like to knock down those who are on top. I think it stems from the fact that we declared we wanted to kick out the British in 1776. We dislike the establishment, the rich, the pompous, the ungrateful, and those who think they are better than us; and we like to feel better about ourselves by laughing at those who are morally or ethically worse than we are.

If I could dream up the ideal story to cross my desk, it would be one about a member of the Royal Family marrying a Kardashian who is impregnated by Simon Cowell, who then tries to escape the publicity by adopting Honey Boo Boo and taking them both on a honeymoon, being first flown by a drunken airline pilot to New York and then getting on a cruise ship full of norovirus. By the way, norovirus funny, Ebola not.

Is there a common thread here at what we laugh at as a culture? We laugh "up" and "down." We laugh at those who are at the top of society's food chain to bring them to our level and we laugh at those who are beneath us because we are better or smarter than them. And I think for the most part we have a universal common sense. In a nation of 320 million people, 300 million know what's right and wrong and what's dumb or not. When I first started writing for Jay, I looked for ideas that defined his point of view. The best I could come up with was that when Jay walks into a room and looks at something, or reads a story, he says, "What's stupid about this?" That's why Jay was a common voice for all of us. And he did this during times of crisis when we needed reassurance, like after the Northridge earthquake (when you can make fun of the villain, Mother Nature, you own it) and when the government acted in a mind-boggling incompetent or hypocritical way.

Here are some examples of both. The first are the jokes from the night after the earthquake.

WELCOME TO LOS ANGELES. Some assembly required . . .

Now, I want to give you this warning for your own good, you know. This is something you might be interested in. With these aftershocks, this is not a good day to get a vasectomy, okay, guys?

IT WAS PRETTY SCARY . . . You know, I woke up at four thirty in the morning, doors slamming, dishes breaking . . . I thought, How did Shannen Doherty get into my house?

∥∥∥∥∥∥∥∥∥∥

I HAD TO go to the hospital yesterday to get the cat removed from my face. Have you had that . . . Man, the cat went batty! You know, when you watch a cartoon and the cat jumps up and the . . . and goes bing! Oh, I thought they just made that up. It's true! The cat went and ricocheted off the wall and I haven't seen it since.

∥∥∥∥∥∥∥∥∥∥

IN FACT, the quake was so bad, Lyle Menendez's toupee ended up on Erik's head. That's how bad it was. Unbelievable . . .

∥∥∥∥∥∥∥∥∥∥

DID YOU DRIVE around today? The whole city . . . every freeway is like Lex Luthor is trying to capture the town.

IT TOOK FOREVER to get to work this morning. In fact, traffic was backed up for hours. And that was just from the people in LA who are trying to move to Oregon.

|||||||||||

I'M SURE YOU KNOW, LA has been declared a disaster area. For what, the ninth time this year? It's like every month. In fact, a lot of Californians say they want Bill Clinton to come and visit some of the devastated areas. Forget Clinton, let's get Jimmy Carter. At least he knows how to build houses. That's the guy we need. Bring the hammer . . .

And here are some examples of when Jay just lacerated hypocrisy and stupidity in government:

ATTORNEY GENERAL John Ashcroft went on to say that our way of life is being threatened by a group of radical religious fanatics who are armed and dangerous. And then he called for prayers in the schools and an end to gun control.

MORE WARNINGS ISSUED by all branches of the government today that another terrorist attack is imminent. We're not sure when, we're not sure where, just that it is coming. Who is attacking us now, the cable company?

||||||||||||

THE WHITE HOUSE has given permission for a company owned by the government of Dubai to run six US ports, including the Port of New York. Now, Dubai was accused of supporting the September 11 attacks and was one of only three countries to support the Taliban. Now they're going to run the Port of New York. What's next, we'll put Mexico in charge of immigration? How about Dick Cheney in charge of gun safety? Courtney Love in charge of Olympic drug testing?

All great comics say things in their acts that have the audience thinking, *Exactly, I get it. . . . That's my family, too, why didn't I say that. . . .* Or, *I could have been saying that onstage.* The difference is the comic is actually onstage saying it, the comic has the balls to go and do it and risk the humiliation of failing at his job in front of audiences big and small . . . and the comic has the advantage of then building on what was said, twisting it, turning it upside down and inside out, and taking it beyond the universal "What's stupid about this premise?" That is what we laugh at.

And there is one sure universal that we all laugh at—stupid elected officials.

When Jay was the emcee at the Genesis Prize show in Israel and asked me to go with him to help out with some logistics of the show, the first thing I asked the organizers was "Who is the audience?" It was 50 percent Israeli, 25 percent Jewish American, and 25 percent Russian. Good luck finding a common denominator there. This is not a group that is going to know Suge Knight is a really bad driver. But what they do know is that politicians are corrupt. That's true whether you are a Russian Jew or a Saudi Muslim. Although I'm pretty sure there were no Saudis at this event. So we researched which Israeli politicians had gone to jail—a lot in the past few months, it turned out—and we did jokes about them. Perfect—we were topical and universal. Certain jokes even transcend cultures.

But over in Israel I found out one place where cultures differ—American late-night hosts tend to end not with politics but with a sex joke. Not dirty but something light, nothing heavy. Here are the final two jokes at the Genesis Prize show:

I WAS STUNNED at how many former politicians in Israel are in prison. In fact, if you ask a former Israeli politician for their cell number, it has a whole different meaning.

||||||||||||

IN MY HOTEL ROOM last night I turned on the TV and a Jewish porn film was on. I knew it was a Jewish porn film because before the woman had sex with the guy, she took him home to meet her parents. "So what do you do for a living?"

The first one killed, and the second, which would have been big in the US, got moderate laughs. Lesson learned.

According to one study by the Center for Media and Public Affairs, the following were Leno's top-twenty political topics over twenty-two years, and the number of jokes on each. Again, I'm not sure how the bean counters quantified a joke about Gore that had a Clinton punch line, but regardless of the numbers, this matches my general sense of what Jay did:

1. Bill Clinton: 4,607

2. George W. Bush: 3,239

3. Al Gore: 1,026

4. Barack Obama: 1,011

5. Hillary Clinton: 939

6. Dick Cheney: 673

7. Monica Lewinsky: 454

8. Bob Dole: 452

9. John McCain: 426

10. Mitt Romney: 361

11. John Kerry: 357

12. George H. W. Bush: 343

13. Newt Gingrich: 328

14. Sarah Palin: 300

15. Ross Perot: 288

16. Arnold Schwarzenegger: 288

17. Joe Biden: 274

18. Dan Quayle: 260

19. John Edwards: 229

20. Osama bin Laden: 216

It's a little odd that bin Laden made this list, as he wasn't elected. And if he was elected, I'm guessing women didn't vote. Also I'm also guessing he did really badly with the Jewish vote. So I'd replace him with Herman Cain, because there is nothing odder than a pizza shop owner who runs for president so he can harass women.

In terms of pop culture figures the list is as follows:

1. O. J. Simpson: 795
2. Michael Jackson: 505
3. Martha Stewart: 208
4. Paris Hilton: 153
5. Lindsay Lohan: 153
6. Robert Blake: 121
7. Anna Nicole Smith: 55
8. Roger Clemens: 50
9. Tonya Harding: 49
10. Alex Rodriguez: 49
11. Heidi Fleiss: 48
12. Charlie Sheen: 48
13. Lance Armstrong: 47
14. Michael Vick: 47
15. Madonna: 46
16. Justin Bieber: 44
17. Britney Spears: 42

18. Kobe Bryant: 38
19. Chris Brown: 38
20. Kim Kardashian: 37

Now, wait a second, earlier I mentioned Jay was nice to Lindsay. Here's the difference. The jokes that were done were when she was going to jail and crashing her car, not when she was close to a breakdown. Not only that, many of what's categorized as a Lindsay Lohan joke were really jokes about her mother and father and how screwed up they are.

CHAPTER FOUR

Writing the Monologue

Every joke writer has a different approach. Some, like me, go for volume; others write fewer jokes, but each one is a beauty.

Some writers I know learned to write a late-night joke by listening to the monologues and typing them out to get the rhythm. Others (like me) stumbled into it. Basically I started typing and then went back and took out everything on the page that didn't sound like a joke.

Here are a few things you need to know, especially if you are an aspiring joke writer. The font size doesn't matter, nor does double-spacing, single-spacing, or even in my case-perfect speling. What works is to look at what is in the news, succinctly set up a true premise, and then come up with the punch line, or take the premise, do the twist on the joke by changing the premise slightly or taking it to the next step, and then delivering the punch line. If the topic is well known, then you can use it as the joke itself.

SIMPLE SETUP AND JOKE

JUSTIN BIEBER is planning to go on tour in Israel.

Haven't the Jews suffered enough?

SETUP, THEN TWIST AND PUNCH LINE

POLICE IN DALLAS, TEXAS, are looking for three women who robbed a Condoms to Go store. Let's forget the crime for a minute. Condoms to go? That's the name of the store? As opposed to what, condoms you have to use right there in the store? "Sir, you have to use that here . . . you cannot leave the building."

My process was not typically used by other writers but worked for me. I started every day reading *Drudge* and the *Huffington Post* and scanning *USA Today* and the *New York Post*. I would then pick nine big topics of the day. Let's say it is June 13, 2014, when I am writing this, so here are the topics I'd pick today.

Iraq is a mess.

Eric Cantor lost his primary election.

The World Cup is under way.

The NBA Finals are under way.

Immigration reform.

Hillary's book.

Obama approval rating.

Friday the thirteenth.

Rick Perry compares homosexuality to alcoholism.

Now, I could have added Bowe Bergdahl, people learning to talk to monkeys, or a hooker using a public library as her base of operations, but I'm going with nine big stories and some secondary ones.

So my first batch of jokes are going to be about the big topics, tying them together when I can. It's Friday the thirteenth, could Eric Cantor's luck get any worse?

After I've written thirty to forty jokes on those, I'll hit the secondary topics. These are ones that are fading from the news but are still relevant. Once I have about seventy jokes written I go to *Fark*, a wonderful website that compiles odd stories from around the country. Between that and *TMZ*, I've got my oddball stories and my celebrity news. One hundred jokes are done. Jay eliminates those that are not monologue-worthy, the show gets taped, and I begin again for the next day.

This raises another question I'm always asked—right up there with "What is Jay like?" "Who is the nicest star you ever met?" and "Why do you insist on having a rolled-up sock in your pants pocket?"—and that question is, Do you ever get writer's block? The answer is, Actually, not really. For two reasons. First, there is a never-ending supply of people doing stupid things around the world who provide a never-ending supply of joke material to mine; and, second, when it's a slow day, you can always warm up and do some formula jokes, "It's so hot, it's so cold . . ." I think these were invented by Johnny Carson. Example: "It's so cold back east, Miley Cyrus twerked a snowman." Not a great joke, not even really a good one, but it's a joke, and once that's typed at the top of a page, then the good ones start to flow.

Here is a sample monologue that Jay did on the night of October 21, 2013. Why am I having you look at this particular monologue? I had just won five dollars in the lottery playing the numbers 10 21 13. Keep in mind that this was at the height of the Obamacare website debacle, and the Dodgers had just choked.

KIND OF A ROUGH DAY today. A friend of mine was given six months by his doctor. Not to live, to sign up for Obamacare.

||||||||||||

I'VE GOT TO ADMIT, I don't quite understand how the whole Obamacare thing works. Like the other day I got a flu shot, but it was from a drone. Like they are combining different elements of the government . . .

||||||||||||

THE PRESIDENT SPOKE today about it; regarding the Obamacare website glitches. The president said he is bringing in "the best and the brightest" to solve the problem. Here's my question: Why didn't he bring in the best and the brightest in the first place? This is typical Washington. They only bring in the best and the brightest as a last resort.

||||||||||||

YOU KNOW WHAT'S going to happen once they bring in the best and the brightest . . . more American jobs lost to India. There you go right there!

THE PRESIDENT was very blunt this afternoon. He said, "There's no sugarcoating the problems with the health care website." See, that's a mistake, we're Americans, we love sugarcoating. If you sugarcoat something, Americans will buy it. The more sugar, the better. In fact, sugar is the reason we have Obamacare in the first place. . . .

||||||||||||

HERE'S A GREAT STORY. The *New York Post* says that Arnold Schwarzenegger wants to change the Constitution so he can run for president. I think that's what he said, that he wants to run for president. . . . Either that or he said, "I'd like to brush with Pepsodent."

That's what the article said; Arnold wants to change the Constitution so he can run for president. Which is the complete opposite of what most politicians do: they get elected president and then they change the Constitution. That's how it's usually done.

If you think Obamacare is controversial, wait until we have Arnoldcare. What will Arnoldcare be like? Health coverage for all pregnant housekeepers? Who's going to go for that?

|||||||||||

DID YOU HEAR about this boy? Boy, this is unbelievable. The L.A. Dodgers are offering Clayton Kershaw a $300 million contract. Imagine how much more he'd get if he could beat the Cardinals? How much more would that be?

Three hundred million dollars! How do you even negotiate that? "I will give you $280 million . . ." "Come on! The man's got to eat!"

|||||||||||

THE MAYOR of Montebello, California, told the *LA Times* she was shocked to learn that her husband was arrested for running a meth lab. She said she had no clue—every house has six thousand packets of Sudafed, don't they? Of course! Flu season is coming.

|||||||||||

DID YOU SEE this story? To protect himself from nosy people moving into his neighborhood up in Palo Alto, Facebook's Mark Zuckerberg spent $30 million buying all the houses around him. I guess he's afraid of strangers. They might steal the most intimate details of his private life and then sell them to the highest bidder. Wouldn't want to have that . . .

|||||||||||

NESTLÉ CORPORATION is now looking to sell off the dieting company Jenny Craig. They say it's not profitable enough. They say one of the problems is that, in this economy, people can't afford to buy all the prepackaged meals. See, that's what I love about America. This is the only place in the world where a bad economy and lack of money cause you to gain weight. How does that work? There is no other country in the world . . . only in America can you be broke and get fatter. . . . You know why? 'Cause we sugarcoat everything. That's why! We need more sugarcoating.

|||||||||||

HERE'S A VERY creepy story. A TSA federal air marshal has been arrested after being accused of snapping "upskirt" cell phone pictures of women as they boarded a flight in Nashville. How creepy is that? The TSA said they are considering whether to suspend the guy. What's to consider: He was a bad photographer? What? The pictures are blurry? We can't make these photos out . . . look how blurry that is.

IIIIIIIIIII

A WOMAN HERE in Los Angeles gave birth to a baby boy inside a Barnes & Noble store. You know what that means? For the first time ever there were two people in a bookstore in LA. That has never happened.

IIIIIIIIIII

HERE'S A HAPPY STORY. A couple in Paraguay who have been living together for eighty years finally got married. In fact, on the honeymoon they both slipped into something more comfortable—a coma.

IIIIIIIIIII

SUPERMODEL BAR REFAELI—she's been here—remember Bar Refaeli? Beautiful . . . *Sports Illustrated*, one of the most beautiful women in the world. She told an Israeli newspaper that she can't understand why she can't find a boyfriend. She says she's simply looking for someone who is "big, strong, and famous." You know there are only so many of us to go around. I'm married. Tom Brady is married. That's pretty much it.

|||||||||||

A NEW STUDY has found that materialism and money can destroy marriages. Do you need a study for that? Can't you just watch *Keeping Up with the Kardashians*? Doesn't that make it fairly obvious?

I guess you heard that story, that Bruce Jenner and Kris Jenner have broken up. In fact, now that Bruce is single, he's getting his own reality show called *Here Comes Honey Bruce Bruce*.

A good solid monologue. Now, here are jokes that almost made the cut, that were in at one thirty p.m., but were cut before Jay went onstage at four.

ACCORDING TO a new survey from public-policy polling, Americans have a higher opinion of hemorrhoids than they do of Congress. And unfortunately Obamacare can only get rid of one of those.

I LOVE THIS story. Officials in Seattle want to know why a detective working undercover at strip clubs spent $16,835 buying 130 lap dances without making a single arrest. In fact, not only did he spend over $16,000 on lap dances, his dry-cleaning bill was over $30,000.

||||||||||

THE TANNING MOM . . . remember her? She has made a porn film. I guess this is for the guys who are into leather.

The Tanning Mom shot a porn video. I understand it's being used to treat guys who have an erection that lasts for more than four hours.

||||||||||

A NEW STUDY says that 12 percent of young moms are on their phones during sex. On their phone! How rude is that? How many guys are going, "What, you can't wait two minutes?"

||||||||||

IT TURNS OUT those furloughed government workers will get back pay, and they also get to keep any unemployment benefits they collected. So this wasn't really a government shutdown, it was a paid vacation.

|||||||||||

THIS IS AMAZING. Last week in LA a woman had a baby in a Barnes & Noble. Amazing, last week in LA not one but two people were in a Barnes & Noble.

|||||||||||

REGARDING THE Obamacare glitches, President Obama said he was bringing in "the best and the brightest" to fix the problem. Which raises the question: Why didn't he bring in the best and the brightest in the first place? You know, maybe that's the problem in Washington. They only bring in the best and the brightest as a last resort.

You notice that a few that didn't make the cut are similar to ones that did. That's because different writers often write the same joke with different wording. Jack Coen and Jay would look at them and decide which worked best.

Why did the jokes above not make the show while the others did? Jay read *millions* of jokes to get to the 160,000 that made the air. He picked late-night jokes better than anyone, although as a self-absorbed writer, I would often think, *But he missed the best one on the page.* I would think that but was almost always wrong. That's why I never pitched jokes to him in person. For twenty-two years I let the lines on the page work or not.

So in writing jokes you can see the template: Start with the big story everyone knows—Obamacare, for example—move into secondary stories, and then do the topics that need to be explained in the premise, fill them out with surveys and smaller stories, and end with a sex joke.

What we learned about America if you watched the night of October 21, 2013, was this: that the Obamacare website stank, the Dodgers choked, the TSA is still outrageous, and that the idiot celebrities of the week were the Kardashians.

So that was the monologue that night, just one of the 4,610 monologues that Jay did. Some jokes worked, others didn't. Typical night. But unlike a stand-up comic, whose act involves delivering jokes tried out night after night in clubs, a late-night host must try out his or her jokes for the first time live in front of an audience of tourists and 4 million people watching at home.

Once the monologue is launched, we are done with it. But that's when the reaction to our monologue and to every other late-night show's monologue begins. Radio stations air the monologue as is, and morning news people dissect what was said and repeat the best of. And occasionally someone reacts or, as is the case with the government, finally acts.

In 2012 Jay and other late-nighters did jokes about the GSA junket scandal. Basically, General Services Administration employees took an $823,000 junket to Vegas. The story broke, we did jokes on it, outrage grew, and Federal News Radio summed it up this way: "GSA even made the Jay Leno show joke list—something that federal workers and politicians should avoid at all costs."

Here is one of the jokes we did:

> HERE'S YOUR TAX DOLLARS at work. This is what makes people furious. The head of the GSA, a woman named Martha Johnson, has resigned after they found out she spent over $830,000 on a four-day government conference in Las Vegas. And the president is furious. Not President Obama, the president of China. It's his money.

So the news story broke, late-night writers turned a spotlight on it, the story grew, newscasters then wouldn't let it go, we did more jokes about it because it was in the news every day, outrage grew, Federal News Radio called it "the talk of Washington." Heads rolled, Congress promised a crackdown . . . and nothing really was done, which means next year there will be the same scandal with different names to provide fodder for the next generation of late-night writers. It's the joke circle of life.

JOKES I WISH I HAD WRITTEN

It's not the women I've had sex with that I think about, it's the ones I haven't. I can't remember a lot of my jokes, but I sure remember those of others I wish I had written. Here are a few just from the year 2012:

> Tim Tebow and actress Camilla Belle have called it quits. The rumor is, she caught him not having sex with another woman.
>
> —JAY LENO

> A new survey found that Sophia and Aiden were the most popular baby names this year. The least popular baby name was Kim Jong Sandusky.
>
> —JIMMY FALLON

> Are you sick and tired of hearing the term "fiscal cliff"? People don't understand it. It doesn't tell you how serious the situation is. They need more color-

ful metaphors. Here's how to explain it: "It's four a.m. for our economy, and Lindsay Lohan is behind the wheel."

—JAY LENO

David Petraeus was reportedly not well liked at the CIA, where he worked. A tip to you fellows out there—don't cheat on your wife if you work with professional spies who don't like you.

—CONAN O'BRIEN

I knew Obama was going to win. I knew this little secret. Use it next time there is an election and see if it doesn't work out. The guy who wins the presidential election is usually the guy who kills bin Laden.

—DAVID LETTERMAN

The movie *Cloud Atlas* opens today. Tom Hanks is in it. In *Toy Story*, he played a cowboy. In *Saving Private Ryan*, he played a soldier. In *Cast Away*, he played a shirtless hairy dude. If he plays a Native American, he'll have achieved something called The Village People Grand Slam.

—CRAIG FERGUSON

After months of dating, this week Taylor Swift broke up with her boyfriend, Conor Kennedy. And when Kennedy asked if they were ever getting back together, Taylor just handed him an iPod and said, "Play track six."

—JIMMY FALLON

Donald Trump was bumped from speaking at the Republican convention because of Hurricane Isaac. See, nobody ever talks about the good things hurricanes do.

—JAY LENO

Tough Olympic news for the Romneys. Ann Romney's horse Rafalca did not advance to the Olympic finals. Apparently it was beat by a smooth-talking socialist horse from Kenya.

—CONAN O'BRIEN

It's not such a great day for fans of the game show *Jeopardy*. Alex Trebek says he may retire at the end of the season. Trebek says he wants to spend more time at home, arrogantly correcting his family.

—CRAIG FERGUSON

Over the weekend Betty White endorsed Barack Obama. I think I'm going to wait and hear what Angela Lansbury has to say.

—DAVID LETTERMAN

Time magazine has come out with their hundred most influential people issue, and Newt Gingrich is not on the list. In fact, he's not even on the list of the hundred most influential Newts.

—JAY LENO

It looks like Kanye West and Kim Kardashian are dating, and apparently they're getting serious. Friends say Kanye is the man Kim wants to spend the rest of her month with.

—JAY LENO

Mitt Romney said that he liked to fire people. Well, there's a pretty good message to send to Middle America. When Rick Perry heard that, he said, "Well, that's nothing. I like to execute people."

—DAVID LETTERMAN

Two points: I wish I had written each of them; and they are all good. Take the names off and not one stands out as edgier on one end or more obvious than the others; a good joke is a good joke.

Bill James, the legendary baseball numbers guru, described players as having peak value and career value. Sandy Koufax with his five brilliant years in the early sixties had peak value as a pitcher. The Phillies' Ryan Howard had it for about five years. Greg Maddux, who was great year after year over a long time, had peak value. It is the same for joke topics. There are people who for a few short weeks or even a year were monologue staples, regardless of who the late-night host was: the tanning mom, Kato Kaelin, Chris Brown, Ross Perot, the runaway bride, Warren Jeffs, Elian Gonzalez, the diaper-wearing jealous female astronaut, Lance Armstrong, Nancy "Why Me" Kerrigan, and Donald Sterling. And then there are people who through either their position (any president counts here) or their repeated screwups (thank God for Charlie Sheen) have great career value. Hillary Clinton may not be topical this week or month but she is always and permanently relevant, and has been and will be a good topic for jokes for years to come. The key is to mine them during their peak value until their gold runs out; when they have career value, appreciate them and use them judiciously, preferably when they have emerged from their cocoon to make news again.

A JOKE TOO FAR

What is a joke too far? It's a phrase comedy writers use about a joke we know will offend. It's the one that you write to push the boundary. It's funny, but you know it's not going to get in. It's funny, but it can't be said because it's too mean, or too soon. Unless it's by the right comic. An example: On Letterman, right after the Eric Garner tragedy, Chris Rock was on the show promoting *Top Five* (great movie, a must-see) and the musical guest was Sting. Chris said, "I saw Sting backstage. Threw up my hands, scared of the Police!" Chris can do that, that's not a joke too far for him; but if another comic had done that, it might have been a joke too far or too soon. Chris has always been willing to push things. In fact, he said he is not playing college campuses anymore because students are too sensitive and unable to take jokes, they are too unwilling to offend.

Which brings me to Sony and their initial cave-in on *The Interview*. Totally spineless. As we used to say in law school, hard cases make bad law. Yes, I understand that people were scared of the threats. Yes, I understand Sony felt it had an obligation to stockholders. But until they flip-flopped, they had opened Pandora's box so that anyone can be blackmailed. Sony should have given a big fat middle finger to whoever hacked them. Jon Stewart was brilliant in pointing out that the nation that said post-9/11 that we never back down let Kim Jong-un decide what movies we can see. Was the movie good? I don't know. Did the movie offend with a joke? Yes. Was it a joke too far? No. The only one who went too far was Sony in bending over backward from day one.

Now, since I am pro First Amendment (I make Justices William Douglas and Hugo Black look like Scalia and Rehnquist), what do I think about horrific racist things people put on the Internet? Disgusting and horrific, they are not even jokes too far as they are not jokes, they are hate speech. But in the end, should we censor? No. Instead we should use our jokes and humor to call them out, shine the spotlight on them, and make fun of them. Because in the end, once we are laughing at someone and their ignorance, they begin to lose their power. And that power of laughter as a leveler has been true whether it was Charlie Chaplin in *The Great Dictator,* Jack Benny in *To Be or Not to Be,* or Leno and Letterman and Stewart taking on bin Laden and al-Qaeda.

THE PERFECT JOKE STORM

To me, the funny events that work best are those that result when giant entities we don't like screw up, but never so seriously that anyone gets hurt. NASA putting in the wrong O-ring in a space shuttle is not a good topic. But a drunken airline pilot landing safely at the wrong airport? Bingo! Same goes for a Carnival cruise ship adrift at sea when hundreds of people are projectile-vomiting while enjoying explosive diarrhea.

JOKE RUNS

We named these "Rodney runs" after Dangerfield. The setup would be something like "It's so hot that . . . ," "It's so cold that . . . ," "The economy is so bad that . . ." I loved these runs. It was a way to get in a lot of jokes in a short time that were there just for the laughs (hot/cold) or made a point . . . that the government was screwing up and that the economy was bad.

Here's an example of a joke run on the economy from 2012:

THE ECONOMY IS SO BAD . . .

THE STOCK MARKET is going down faster than a general's biographer.

||||||||||||

ON THE WAY to work I saw Phil Jackson holding up a sign: "Will coach for food."

||||||||||||

JAMES BOND SWITCHED from Heineken to Colt 45.

||||||||||||

PAULA BROADWELL IS now being forced to sleep with only three-star generals.

||||||||||||

MSNBC HAD TO lay off three hundred Obama spokesmen.

||||||||||||

PRESIDENT OBAMA SENT Susan Rice out to defend it.

Those last two jokes are why Jay was different than other late-night hosts; more nights than the others, he made fun of a Democratic president.

THE HIDDEN TRUTH

One writer who for many years wrote for Jay and also wrote for Dave Letterman is Wayne Kline. Wayne always said, "We don't write jokes, we just rewrite the news." I think of it more as just telling the truth, but with an amplifier.

HERE IS AN EXAMPLE OF A PERFECT HIDDEN-TRUTH JOKE:

A WOMAN WAS ARRESTED for actually cooking meth inside a Walmart. The worst part, the meth was the only item in that Walmart made in America.

Why does that joke work? Because it's true and we know it and we're scared at what it says, so we laugh at it to relieve our tension. And maybe that's the greatest gift any late-night-show host can give his audience.

CHAPTER FIVE

How Late Night Gives Us the News

Johnny gave us the modern late-night show. Jay took it to the next level in 1992. Jay almost doubled the length of Johnny's monologue and, in addition to covering the full array of news and pop culture events, did jokes about politics that went much deeper than anything Johnny had ever done. He was groundbreaking, paving the way for the Jon Stewarts, Bill Mahers, Stephen Colberts, and John Olivers of today. And Jay was perfect for the age of twenty-four-hour news. With the proliferation of cable and the rise and influence of Matt Drudge and of gossip websites, "we the people" suddenly knew a little about everything. Or maybe we were so busy, we really didn't know anything about anything. Either way, we needed someone to give us a definitive take on the news.

Jay summed up his approach to the monologue when he said: "People are busy, work hard, they may have missed the news, so you have to give them a complete view of the news."

That's what Jay did. His monologue would take on the biggest topic of the day, the political news, the sports news, the celebrity gossip, the science news, and the odd stories that we all had heard about . . . Or if we hadn't, Jay told us about them, whether it was the mom in Alabama who drove with her kids strapped to the roof of her car or the most expensive coffee in the world, made by passing coffee beans through the digestive tract of a civet cat. True story—which explains their slogan: "See what brown can do for you."

But are late-night shows really giving people the news? For a long time I had heard anecdotally from college students and professors I knew that more and more people were getting the news from late night. And, being skeptical (the third most important attribute of a comedy writer, right behind having an extremely twisted mind and a desire never to pay for one's own lunch), I would note that the plural of *anecdote* is not *data*. But then the data came in.

A 2004 poll by the Pew Research Center for the People and the Press (you would think they would change the name from

"Pew") found that 21 percent of people between the ages of eighteen and twenty-nine cited *The Daily Show* and *Saturday Night Live* as the sources where they regularly learned presidential campaign news. That was up from 9 percent in 2000. Even more startling, in that same time period the percentage of young people who got their campaign news from ABC, CBS, or NBC declined from 39 percent to 23 percent.

Has this continued? Will this continue? I think so.

Even though the new landscape of late night is changing, people will still watch for the same reasons they always did—to get a take on the events of the day. And here is the scary part: it's a take they can trust. Decades ago people believed in the news broadcasters. Walter Cronkite was the most trusted man in America. Now we have a cynical view of those institutions and those who work for them. According to a June 2014 Gallup poll, public confidence in television news is at an all-time low, and only 18 percent of Americans said they have a "great deal" or "quite a lot" of confidence in that news medium. In 1993 it was 46 percent, and now it's down to 18 percent! To put that in perspective, 19 percent of Americans trust their local drug dealer. As well they should. Especially after the Brian Williams debacle.

Think about it. Fox and MSNBC don't report news, they give opinions. CBS, ABC, and NBC are dinosaurs, and CNN can't get anything right. Remember their rush to give the wrong information on the Boston Marathon bombing and the Supreme Court decision on Obamacare?

Meanwhile, Obama White House press secretary Jay Carney said in a talk at George Washington University: "I remember we had some discussion during 2012 whether it is appropriate for the president, the sitting president and candidate, to give interviews with Jon Stewart and others. And the answer was yes, again because the young voters we were trying to reach are more likely to watch *The Daily Show* than some other news shows. But also, I think if you look back at 2012 and the series of interviews the sitting president of the United States gave, probably the toughest interview he had was with Jon Stewart. Probably the most substantive, challenging interview Barack Obama had in the election year was with the anchor of *The Daily Show*."

So where we used to watch the monologues of late night in the sixties, seventies, and eighties to be entertained, in the nineties and the first decade of the twenty-first century the late-night monologues gave us our *take* on the news and now we consider them a source *where we actually get the news*. Which means that each joke and each late-night show shapes the way we look at events, at celebrities, and, perhaps even more important, at our political leaders.

WHAT A MONOLOGUE CAN . . . AND CAN'T DO

A late-night monologue (and for brevity I'll use that term to include sketches you see on *SNL* or a top-ten list or any comedy bit after eleven p.m. EST) can't convince the audience of something that it doesn't already know or suspect. A joke whose punch line suggests that Stephen Hawking is dumb won't work; a top-ten list that tries to portray Lance Bass as a ladies' man won't work, either.

Jokes have to connect with what we already believe, what's in the zeitgeist, or what makes sense, based on our experience. Audiences are smart. They let you know what is believably funny.

In 2008 I was brought in to help with Obama debate prep. I was brought in for a combination of reasons: (1) I had twelve years' experience doing debate prep from my political days; (2) the key to debate prep is using the opponent's setup to deliver your own punch line (remember Lloyd Bentsen's brilliant response to Dan Quayle's JFK comparison—by the way, not my line, although I wish it had been); and (3) campaign guru David Axelrod is a longtime friend who took me to my one and only Bulls play-off game. At one point during the campaign I told Axe that a late-night studio audience was a pretty effective focus group. I could tell from their reaction to jokes about Obama versus jokes about McCain who was up and who was down. Not only that, you could also see the change a week or so ahead of when the poll numbers would start to climb or fall.

The key to divining the current status or future prospects of a candidate (or celebrity) is when the audience laughs at the mere mention of the name instead of waiting for the joke. When you are the punch line, when you got caught with a hooker named Divine Brown and people laugh at the mention of just your first name, that's when you better do some serious damage control to address the problem (more on Hugh Grant later).

In September 2008, during the GOP convention, Barack Obama's numbers started to drop and John McCain was moving into the lead. Clearly a post-convention bounce, right? Except that a few days before the GOP convention, the laughter about Obama and Biden was getting a bit louder every night. The sense of unease the country may have had about the possibility of a "community organizer from Kenya" (as Donald Trump might describe him) in the White House caused people to give Obama a long, hard look.

Watching our studio audience react and listening to their laughter, I just knew people were starting to worry about the prospect of Barack Obama as president. And I'm not talking about your Idaho voters in Sandpoint storing guns and provisions for the day the movie *Red Dawn* became a documentary. I'm talking about real middle-of-the-road, average Americans. The jokes about whether he was ready to handle the job were scoring. I remember calling Axe, and he told me that their polls were reflecting a slight erosion. The audience thermometer had worked again. Then, a few days later, Lehman Brothers collapsed, the stock market cratered, John McCain announced the economy was fundamentally sound, and the Obama rocket was ready for launch.

Let's think about that. With that one statement about the economy in the wake of a stock market collapse, the political pundits had what they needed, a way to say McCain was old and out of touch without saying he was old. It was a way to get to him about his judgment, which, combined with his pick of Sarah Palin, evened the playing field. You no longer had the inexperienced community organizer from Kenya (I'm kidding!) versus the seasoned pro who would have a steady hand on the tiller that guided the ship of state. Instead you had someone saying, "We have a problem and I have the energy to fix it," versus a befuddled guy who said, "What problem?"

Here is the avalanche that comment started:

He looks like a guy who's backed over his own mail-box. He looks like the guy at the supermarket who is confused by the automatic doors. He looks like the guy at the movies whose wife has to repeat everything.

—DAVID LETTERMAN

Today John McCain campaigned in the Ohio town of Defiance. Next comes Anger, then finally Acceptance.

—JAY LENO

McCain suspended his campaign, said the debate had to be canceled, he went to Washington, screwed up the deal, and then un-suspended his campaign and flew to the debate even though there wasn't a deal. Usually when a seventy-two-year-old man acts this way, this is when the kids start calling nursing homes.

—BILL MAHER

A woman at a John McCain rally said that Barack Obama is an Arab. And McCain quickly corrected her. It was really awkward, because McCain had to tell her, "Look, Governor Palin, you are wrong."

—JAY LENO

This doesn't smell right. This is not the way a tested hero behaves. Somebody's putting something in his Metamucil.

—DAVID LETTERMAN,
*on John McCain's canceling his appearance
on* Late Show with David Letterman

It got a little heated at one point during the debate. McCain talked about experience and he said, "We don't have time for on-the-job training." Then why did you pick Sarah Palin?

—JAY LENO

Barack Obama is actually going door-to-door, knocking on doors in a neighborhood, asking people if they'll vote for him. Coincidentally, John McCain is also going door-to-door, except when he knocks on a door, he says, "Do I live here?"

—DAVID LETTERMAN

Barack Obama said today that he is going to fight for votes in all fifty states. Yeah. That's what he said. Meanwhile, John McCain said he's going to fight for votes in all thirteen colonies.

—CONAN O'BRIEN

John McCain may be behind, but the man is a fighter. He doesn't know the meaning of the word *quit*. He used to, but it was stored in the same part of his brain that remembered to vet his running mate.

—STEPHEN COLBERT

So jokes are a thermometer, but they are also a thermostat. If a person or event is a blank canvas and each late-night host is using his monologue to paint that canvas, then those jokes and shows are creating opinions about people and events, not just reflecting what is out there already. The jokes are conveying information to the public whether it is accurate or not. The lines and sketches are telling people, "This is who this person is, this is what happened, this is what we should collectively think." Look at what happened to Richard Jewell. Remember him—he was the innocent who everyone thought was the mastermind of the 1996 Olympic Park bombing in Atlanta.

WHAT ARE THE WORDS YOU CAN SAY?

Not only can late-night shows change our minds about people and events, they also have an impact on the words that are acceptable to use. For example, before 1993 it was apparently illegal in this country to say the word *penis* in public unless you were a urologist, a twelve-year-old boy on the playground, or Dr. Ruth.

Then in June of that year I was sitting at my desk and the phone rang. It was a political consultant whom I had met once back in my days in DC; he had heard through the grapevine that I was writing for Jay and told me he saw a story in the *Washington Post* Metro section about a woman who had severed her husband's "member" and thrown it out the window of her car. The couple were John Wayne and Lorena Bobbitt, and the consultant asked me if I thought it was joke-worthy. Bingo! He faxed me the clipping (yes, it was that long ago). The story made the evening news—albeit without the word *penis*—and we all began writing jokes. The big question was whether we could use the word *penis* in a joke. I think comedy writers had a collective epiphany and decided *penis* is a funny word, why not? So we did. The world did not end and I believe the next night Dan Rather used the word *penis* on the *CBS Evening*

News. Next thing you know, there is a play called *The Vagina Monologues*, all decorum breaks down, we invade Iraq, cats are lying down with dogs, we get ready to invade Iraq again, and Lena Dunham has her own award-winning show. . . . The point is that once the late-night hosts used the word, it seemed safe for everyone, including Dan Rather and your Aunt Minnie, to use it.

As they say, the jokes wrote themselves. John Wayne Bobbitt is separated, he is currently unattached, and when asked why she did it, he says he's stumped.

Which brings me to answer some criticism of late-night hosts. Critics, of which there are 300 million in America, say they take a subject and do obvious jokes. Yes, they do . . . and they also do really smart ones that are not obvious. People, it's not easy for hosts. Depending on the host, it's fifteen to thirty new jokes a night. Writers call it feeding the monster. We feed it all day, it digests a thousand jokes, and then it's hungry again the next day. Not every joke is going to be a winner, and you have to do it night after night. I'm not saying it's rocket science or as hard as working in a coal mine, but like Hyman Roth said, it's the life we chose. Checking out what's in the news and writing jokes. That's the job. And the joke that didn't make you laugh made someone else laugh.

Now, as fluffers say after lunch break on the movie set, back to the penis. Late-night hosts have always faced the dilemma of how to frame a joke about an awkward subject using words that for a long time were not allowed. One of the most famous incidents was in 1960, when *Tonight Show* host Jack Paar told an incredibly long joke (more like a novel) about a mix-up involving the initials WC, which in England stands for "water closet." After the show, NBC's censors—and by the way, censors are usually actually funny, foulmouthed, and incredibly sexy; the type who would be in their control room bleeping out the word *breast* while having an assistant rub their nipples—cut the joke, Jack got mad, and walked off the show for a month before returning. Here it is, a joke too far in 1960:

An English lady, while visiting Switzerland, was looking for a room, and she asked the schoolmaster if he could recommend any to her. He took her to see several rooms, and when everything was settled, the lady returned to her home to make the final preparations to move.

When she arrived home, the thought suddenly occurred to her that she had not seen a WC [water closet, a euphemism for toilet] around the place. So she immediately wrote a note to the schoolmaster asking him if there was a WC around. The [Swiss] schoolmaster was a very poor student of English, so he asked the [Swiss] parish priest if he could help in the matter. Together they tried to discover the meaning of the letters WC, and the only solution they could find for the letters was Wayside Chapel. The schoolmaster then wrote to the English lady the following note:

"Dear Madam: I take great pleasure in informing you that the WC is situated nine miles from the house you occupy, in the center of a beautiful grove of pine trees surrounded by lovely grounds. It is capable of holding 229 people and it is open on Sunday and Thursday only. As there are a great number of people and they are expected during the summer months, I would suggest that you come early: although there is plenty of standing room as a rule. You will no doubt be glad to hear that a good number of people bring their lunch and make a day of it; while others who can afford to go by car arrive just in time. I would especially recommend that Your Ladyship go on Thursday, when there is a musical accompaniment. It may interest you to know that my daughter was married in the WC, and it was there that she met her husband. I can remember the rush there was for seats. There were ten people to a seat ordinarily occupied by one. It was wonderful to see the expression on their faces. The newest attraction is a bell donated by a wealthy resident of the district. It rings every time a person enters. A bazaar is to be held to provide plush seats for all the people, since they feel it is a long-felt need. My wife is rather delicate, so she can't attend regularly. I shall be delighted to reserve the best seat for you if you wish, where you will be seen by all. For the children, there is a special time and place so that they will not disturb the elders. Hoping to have been of service to you, I remain, Sincerely, the Schoolmaster."

Wow! That wasn't a joke, that was *War and Peace*. Can you imagine doing a joke that long today? They'd have canceled Jack halfway through the joke. Jack came back a month later but that might have sealed his fate, for soon after, he left the show for good, paving the way for King Carson. Silly as this may seem, Jack's using the initials WC in 1960 opened up the door for late-night hosts to use the words *oral sex* on TV in 1998.

To this day, one of the great TV-watching moments in my life was not the moon landing, the Berlin Wall coming down, or Mandela being freed. It was seeing CNN's Candy Crowley, a superb journalist, read the Starr report when it came out and watching her try to keep it together as she talked about stained dresses, cigars, and oral in the Oval Office.

CHAPTER SIX

Politicians

WHY THEY NEED LATE-NIGHT TV

As funny as Johnny's jokes were, they weren't sharp or edgy-political like those of Bill Maher or as political in sheer numbers as Jay's.

S. Robert Lichter, director of the Center for Media and Public Affairs at George Mason University, said that "Johnny Carson initiated political humor on late night, but Leno put it on steroids. Leno always told far more political jokes than anyone else. With folks like Fallon and others, you've got political humor when something big happens . . . so, for Fallon, politics is just one of many areas. For Leno, it was a major part of his arsenal."

And in twenty-two years we had a gigantic arsenal, because

there were so many targets on both sides of the aisle. Unlike Colbert, Stewart, and Maher, Jay never showed his personal side. Jay's theory was always that the emperor, regardless of party, has no clothes. Christian Toto, assistant editor at the conservative news site *Breitbart*, said Leno understood the late-night rule of making fun of the president no matter the party. He said, "Leno was talking truth to power, and it was resonating."

Democrats in the Clinton years thought Jay was a Republican, and Republicans in the Bush years thought he was a Democrat; it's all about whose ox is being gored. The numbers bear this out. Jay did 160,000 jokes over the years, and, according to the Center for Media and Public Affairs, there were more than 20,000 political jokes: 10,885 were about Democrats and 9,465 about Republicans. The slight imbalance is based on the facts that Democrats held the White House thirteen of his twenty-two years and that one of the Democrats inserted a cigar into a chubby Jewish girl.

How did I handle that? I'm a Democrat. I love Bill Clinton. I worked for him, wrote for him at times, think he was an amazing and great president, one of the ten greatest ever. Maybe even in the top seven. But in comedy, I don't care about any of that. You can't ignore that incident. There are things that are close, but no cigar. He didn't inhale, but he did impale.

What we can joke about has changed over the years when it comes to our leaders. Homophobic Idaho senators are caught foot-tapping in an airport men's room, trying to pick up men (Larry Craig—narrow mind, wide stance); congressmen are caught on video making out with their cosmetologist schedulers; presidential candidates cheat on their dying wives with strumpets. A New York mayoral candidate is sending women photos to prove beyond a shadow of a doubt that Anthony Weiner is Jewish. We are seeing a side of politicians we have never seen before . . . generally their front side or back side, with their pants around their ankles. We're inundated with information daily, and no one knows how to process it all. We're being alerted to a new breaking story every few seconds on our e-mail or cell phone, so the handful of events that late-night comics focus on matter simply because they make it into the monologue. In the old days a bunch of old white men at the *Encyclopaedia Britannica* would determine what were facts, and we grew up with a Caucasian-centric Western-civ view. As wrong and as biased as they often were, at least someone was in charge of determining what was important and what was a "fact." Now there's the Internet, where everyone has an opinion, and Wikipedia, where anyone can try to factualize an opinion. Curating those five hundred stories of interest a day is now the responsibility of a late-night host and his head writer, who determine the twenty-five that we will hear, based on this tried and true process:

1. Is it funny? If yes, go to 2.
2. Is it topical? If yes, go to 4; if not, go to 3.
3. If it is not topical, is it in the recent zeitgeist or easily explained? If not, stop; if yes, go to 4.
4. Is it monologue-worthy and a top-of-the-line joke? If yes, insert; if no, go to 5.
5. Is it funny even if not typical of a monologue joke? If so, insert; if not, go to 6.
6. Does it sound funny? Yes, there are jokes that if you pause and reflect on them make you think, *Yeah, I laughed, but I'm not sure why.* The reason is because they sound funny, they sound like a joke. Or because their telling is clever. This joke "type" is just a fact, yet it always got a laugh:

LET ME TELL YOU how the world economy has changed. It's when a Spanish-speaking Mexican living in LA drives his Japanese car to work in a factory owned by Koreans so that he can pay taxes to a government in debt to China that is run by a president born in Hawaii to a Kenyan dad and a Kansas mom.

No one in 1860 knew Lincoln was depressed or once shared a bed with a man; no one knew in 1960 that JFK would have had sex with the crack of dawn; but in 1992 we knew that something had emerged from the trailer parks named Gennifer Flowers. And Jay was there to poke fun at it. We live with the stupidity of our leaders; laughing at them is our chance to punish them.

The jokes may also play another role; they may actually in a strange way help a politician in trouble. Take Bill Clinton and the Lewinsky story. Every late-night comic went to town night after night with each new revelation. Yet Bill Clinton left office with the highest approval rating of any president in modern history. My longtime friend and legendary political consultant Paul Begala has a theory I subscribe to: The late-night comics got it right; it was Congress that got it wrong. Washington, DC, overreacted, they tried to impeach a president over a blow job. If guys were consistently fired over blow jobs, American's unemployment rate would be 69 percent (yes, pun intended). Most Americans got that this whole thing was silly, that it was funny, that it was something to laugh at, and that late-night comics, by making jokes about it, extracted the correct "punishment" on a very good man who did what some believe is a bad thing. Yes, the jokes hurt the family; yes, they made Hillary and Chelsea feel bad. But if Congress had just let it go at that instead of paralyzing the government with an impeachment, we all would have been better off. I think Americans understood this, which is why Bill Clinton today enjoys an approval rating of 69 percent. There's that number again. Maybe Barack Obama and Congress should all get blow jobs from interns, it can't make things any worse.

This reminds me of one of my favorite jokes of 2013. It was in the middle of the Obamacare launch debacle and Rob Ford's crack admissions.

THE LATEST POLLS show President Obama's approval rating down to 39 percent. And Toronto mayor Rob Ford's approval rating went up to 49 percent. How does this make Obama feel? He's better off smoking crack than passing Obamacare.

The experts say that Jay told more than 4,600 jokes about Bill Clinton. Add in what the other hosts told, and it's probably upward of 7,500. Given that it's tough for me to pick my favorite one or ten or hundred, here are a few.[*]

President Clinton has got an office a couple of blocks from here. It's a great location, right between a Wendy's and a Hooters. . . . It's a fabulous building, over on Fifty-seventh Street—Hump Tower . . . He's on the fifty-sixth floor of this office building. What a view! He can see the East River. He can see Central Park. He can see the Hudson River. He can see Hillary coming.

—DAVID LETTERMAN

Yesterday was Earth Day, and President Bush planted some seeds. See, that's the difference between Bush and Clinton. Clinton was a much bigger environmentalist. He didn't just plant his seeds one day, he planted them every day.

—JAY LENO

---

[*]By the way, a thanks to a man I never met, Daniel Kurtzman, the editor of politicalhumor.about.com, who has compiled and made available thousands of late-night political jokes over the years.

President Clinton wants to buy a condo here in Manhattan. I'm thinking, Just pray to God he doesn't buy the place above you. In the middle of the night, you could hear that two-hundred-pound intern drop to her knees.

—DAVID LETTERMAN

Former President Clinton's dog, Buddy, got run over recently. Very sad. Hillary said today she feels terrible, because she was aiming at Bill.

—JAY LENO

Ari Fleischer apologized this week for statements that implied that Bill Clinton's failed peace plan was to blame for the current Mideast violence. What is wrong with these Republicans? Let's go over the Clinton administration again. He did this [shows picture of Monica Lewinsky]. He didn't do this [the word violence appears]. He did this [shows picture of Monica Lewinsky]. He didn't do this [shows the Enron symbol]. He did this [shows picture of Monica Lewinsky]. He didn't do this [shows a chart of the Dow Jones going down]. He did this [shows picture of Monica Lewinsky]. He didn't do this [shows picture of Hillary Clinton].

—TINA FEY

More evidence that the ice shelf down there on the South Pole is breaking up after 50 million years. The Clintons are staying together, but the ice shelf is breaking up. Go figure that out.

—DAVID LETTERMAN

Wes Craven was actually asked to shoot a film that documented Bill Clinton's last day in office. That's a true story, yeah. Yeah, apparently Craven wanted to call the film, *I Know Who You Did Last Summer.*

—CONAN O'BRIEN

He's got a scandalous past and he's talking about how much he's going to love being in the [Senate] spouses' club. Do you think that makes the male senators feel good? Do you think Senator Orrin Hatch right now is sleeping easy? Do you think Lieberman doesn't think Clinton is going to be sidling on up to Hadassah in the Senate club: "Can

I buy you a Manischewitz?" Believe me, they're nervous.

—JON STEWART

Now, do these jokes add to the partisanship and interparty bickering we've seen in America? I'd go the other way and postulate (I have the law degree, it makes my mom happy when I use some of those big law school words) that the late-night jokes about politicians, regardless of party, can unite us.

Alex Castellanos, a leading GOP strategist, CNN commentator, fellow cigar smoker, and all-around great guy, wrote this:

Comedy and, specifically, late-night talk are central to politics. Our mission in politics is to bring people together to create a governing consensus. In other words, our mission is to unite the herd and bring them together around the greatest possible shared purpose: the success and survival of the herd. One-on-one, each and every one of us is vulnerable. When we wildebeests get together, the odds of our survival improve. It is important to belong to a powerful and purposeful political herd, and laughter helps us achieve that mission. When we laugh together at the same thing, we acknowledge our shared perspective, we admit publicly and emotionally that we look at the world from the same place and see things the same way. We acknowledge, in short, that we are of a herd. That is why late-night talk shows are a critical part of the political process. Late-night talk is the watering hole where all we wildebeests go after a long day, after our work is done, not just to renourish ourselves physically, but to renourish ourselves together as a herd. Think of a political debate, an ancient ritual fought in an electronic coliseum. Who is the alpha dog? Does the audience member end up part of the group in support of the gladiator or backing the lion? When Ronald Reagan said, "I want you to know that also I will not make age an issue of this campaign. I am not going to exploit, for political purposes, my opponent's youth and inexperience," everyone laughed. In that moment, we became part of Ronald Reagan's herd, not Mondale's. Whether it's from Jon Stewart, Carson, or Leno, political humor brings us together as a nation—and in a country that is more divided and polarized than every other, it is one of the few things that can.

As an addendum to Alex's excellent analysis, what Reagan did in essence was use a late-night-style joke to make an important election point, demonstrating the impact humor can have on all of us.

WHY POLS COME ON LATE NIGHT

Why do politicians appear on the same late-night shows that use them for comic fodder? For one thing, it's the perfect format. If you're Senator Doakes and are thinking of running for president, chances are that 95 percent of the people watching *Meet the Press* (1) already know who you are politically, and (2) have already made up their minds.

When you come on a late-night show, the viewers for the most part are likely undecided and/or open-minded. They are watching for entertainment, not to be consciously informed. This isn't the DC Beltway crowd that lives and breathes the partisan talking points, watching a Sunday-morning show or cable news show to see people spew out talking points. Let's face it, seeing Susan Rice give the CIA/White House spin on Benghazi, not a lot of laughs. And if you are an R watching her, you already don't believe her; if you are a D watching her, you are already mouthing the words before she says them. If you are watching *Hannity*, I know who you are. If you are watching

Rachel Maddow, the same. But if you are watching late night, you aren't on either far end, you are in the comfortable middle. Especially if you watch *The Tonight Show*. It has been said of Johnny Carson that he was not only at home in Middle America, he was Middle America. Jay, even though he was from back east, appealed to the "flyover states." Our numbers were always huge in cities like Milwaukee and St. Louis, both in swing states, which is another reason presidential candidates would come on the show. Interestingly, Dave, who was from Indiana, had a much more urban NYC appeal than Jay. So if you are a pol going on a show like Jimmy, Jimmy, or Dave, it's a chance to let a few million undecided voters see you and get a chance to know the answer to the question that ultimately decides elections: Is he or she the type of person I'd like to get a beer with?

Wearing my old political consultant hat, I'd modify that to say that the person most likely to be elected president is the candidate whose staff likes them the most personally and who aren't hired guns. Test it, it never fails. And in the case where both candidates are equally beer-worthy and equally loved or hated by their staffs, it comes down to other factors. In 2000, Bush was more beer-worthy and loved by his staff. No one would ever want a beer with Al Gore, and his staff members were for the most part hired guns, not true believers in the way

Karl "Turd Blossom" Rove was a true believer in W. Only the strong Clinton record kept that election close, and once again shows how ludicrous it was for Gore to run from it.

In the end, whether it's a beer or an aspect of likability, a lot of how we perceive candidates is through jokes; so coming on a late-night show is a way for a candidate to dispel the persona that the jokes have reinforced, and a way to demonstrate that he or she is as normal as we are. And for the few days before they come on and a few days after, chances are the host will be a little easier on them. As Jay has said, you don't invite someone into your house and then insult them.

Both John F. Kennedy and Richard Nixon were on Jack Paar's *Tonight Show*, but to me the true love affair between hosts and candidates started in 1988, after Bill Clinton gave an incredibly long and boring speech (the only one of the kind he ever gave in his life) at the Democratic convention nominating Michael Dukakis.

The speech lasted approximately sixty-seven hours (actually thirty-three minutes), the networks kept cutting away, the drunken conventioneers (redundant, and I know this is true as I was one of them) ignored it, and it didn't get applause until the end, when Bill Clinton said, "In closing." Now, part of the problem was that Bill's subject matter, Michael Dukakis, was a man so mind-numbingly nerdy that his wife used to drink rubbing alcohol in order to face dinner with him. But seeing Bill Clinton give a boring speech is like seeing Ozzie Smith make an error—there's only one in your lifetime.

So Bill decided to remedy it and went on *The Tonight Show* with Johnny Carson. His appearance was so memorable that by the day after the show aired he was declared "politically reha-bilitated" and had moved from the loser of the week to political winner of the week.

How did that come about? Who was genius enough twenty-seven years ago to realize that a late-night show could enable a pol to quickly change the perception about who he was? The answer is the Thomasons, Harry and Linda.

Here is what Harry had to say about it :

We were very upset, you know, that it didn't go well. We knew the press was gonna make mincemeat out of him and people would be making fun of him. So we stewed about it all night—this is a Thursday, you know. Some-time in the wee hours Linda wakes me up after a troubled sleep and said, "Look, he's got to go on the Carson show to make this right," and I said, okay, in the morning I'd work on it. So the next morning I called a publicist who worked for us named David Horowitz, and said, "David, do you know anybody at *The Tonight Show*," and he said,

"Yeah, I know Freddie de Cordova." I said, "I want you to call and ask if Clinton can come on the show," and so about eleven thirty in the morning he called me back and said, "I talked to Freddie de Cordova," who was of course Carson's producer, "and he says Carson has never had a politician on his show in his entire career and he's not going to now." And I said, okay, but sometime after lunch I had another idea and just called Freddie de Cordova back direct and said, "Okay, you've never had a politician on, but what if he comes on and plays the saxophone? This guy's a musician." De Cordova laughed, and said, "I'll get back to you, let me go down the hall and talk to Johnny." And so, a half hour later he called and said, "Okay, he's on the show next Thursday night and he's got to play the saxophone," and I said, "Sure, he's gonna do it, we'll have him here."

And so the next Saturday morning I get a call, and the governor wasn't there, but his staff had had a meeting and the chief of staff had said—he called and he was a very nice guy—but he said, "Harry, I've been talking to the staff and we have decided Clinton should go on *The Tonight Show*, but he's not going to play the saxophone." And I said, "Okay, I've got news for you guys," and explained that there was no choice for him, and he came out to do

The Tonight Show. . . . Linda got a big hourglass and gave it to him and said, "Now, when you walk out on the stage at *The Tonight Show,* he's going to say, 'Well, how you doing, Governor,' and you're just going to pull this out and you're going to set it on the desk." And so we're getting ready and we give him the hourglass when Freddie de Cordova comes running in in a panic and said to us, "Do not let him take that hourglass out there." And we were sort of startled at this, 'cause he was upset, you know, and we said, "Oh, okay, okay," and we took it away from him. So Clinton goes out and sits down, and Carson says, "Well, Governor Clinton, how are you doing," and he takes out an hourglass, plops it on top of the desk. . . . That was a good night for Clinton, and he did play the saxophone with the band.

That was memorable, but not nearly as memorable as four years later, when Clinton was running for president. It was May, and although he was the presumptive nominee, in the general election polls he was a distant third. So Bill went on *Arsenio,* and late-night history was made.

Now, the interesting part is that, according to Leno segment producer Dave Berg, *The Tonight Show* turned down Bill Clinton's original offer to appear wearing shades and playing Elvis

Presley songs on his sax. Berg said, "At the time, we didn't understand the opportunity we had missed. Our only late-night role model was Carson, who had had only a handful of politicians as guests."

Bill Clinton ended up on *Arsenio* because Hillary had seen Hall after the April 1992 Rodney King riots and was impressed by his sensitivity and skill in dealing with a very controversial topic. So she told Bill and top advisers James Carville, Paul Begala, and Mandy Grunwald about it and—here's a shock—Hillary convinced them.

So Clinton was booked, and when Arsenio came back to the dressing room, he said something to Clinton along the lines of "You can't wear that red tie, you look like a city councilman in Paducah." Bill said, "You better get me one," and Arsenio came back with an armful of ties. Paul Begala picked a loud yellow one, Bill put on his shades, got out his sax, and that image on late night conveyed the most important difference between George H. W. Bush and Clinton. You didn't need to know much about health care or "It's the economy, stupid"; what mattered was new versus old, cool versus square. 41 (yes, I know them all so well, I call them by their numbers) is a great man, a real World War II hero, and the last man of the greatest generation to be elected to the highest office in the land. But after *Arsenio*, the election was defined as new versus old, and when that's the choice, we always pick new. The appearance on *Arsenio* was the lightning bolt the Clinton campaign needed, and over time he pulled ahead, won the election, and gave comedy writers everywhere the greatest source of jokes in history.

Did a late-night appearance win the election for Bill Clinton? Not by itself, but combined with the bad economy and Perot taking away enough votes from Bush, it meant victory in November.

We learned our lesson on *The Tonight Show*. Soon after, we had on Jimmy Carter and Paul Simon (my old friend the senator, not the singer), and by 2000 we were a regular destination for candidates. As Dave Berg put it, "Politicians saw late night as an opportunity to come across as regular guys in a way news shows did not afford them." Al Gore and W came on a week before the vote. W put on an Al Gore mask and, on Halloween, Gore came as Frankenstein. Or was it Frankenstein as Gore? I always get confused.

Over the years on *The Tonight Show* there were a lot of memorable moments with political guests. John Kerry arrived riding a motorcycle, George W. Bush gave Jay a painting he had done of him, and President Obama came on fifty-eight days into his first term, making it the first time a president had come on a late-night show while in office.

The worst candidate ever to come on the show was John Edwards. You'd meet him and want to take a shower afterward. Total slime bucket. Jay gave him the perfect lead-in question about how Nancy Pelosi had talked about the need for Congress to work harder and right after that had said she wanted a limited workweek. Edwards, the perceived outsider, had the perfect softball: "That's the problem with Washington." Instead, the lying little condom-allergic weasel paused for a show business eternity while apparently calculating how many superdelegates he would lose if he attacked Nancy Pelosi. He then gave a nonanswer. Right then I knew this guy didn't have what it takes.

Edwards was the least likable of candidates ever on *The Tonight Show*, but on the other hand Fred Thompson was probably the least impressive. What a pair—you had Edwards, who would sleep with anybody, and Thompson, who looked like he was asleep while talking about running for president.

Going on a late-night show gives candidates a chance to show they are likable human beings. Which is hard for them, because, remember, *politics* comes from the Greek words *poly*, which means "many," and *ticks*, which means "bloodsucking leeches."

Shows like Bill Maher's, Jon Stewart's, and Stephen Colbert's are a bit riskier but still have a huge upside.

In fact, there is even something called the Colbert Bump. Colbert himself coined it through this very funny description:

> BEFORE MIKE HUCKABEE came on the *Report*, his presidential campaign was polling at 1 percent. After his appearance, he soared to 3 percent. That's a 300 percent increase after a two-and-a-half-minute interview. If he keeps up that pace between now and the election, he'll be the first candidate ever to get elected with 88,128,000 percent of the vote.

And after Ron Paul, a Texan in the same "crazy uncle in the attic" mold as Ross Perot (what is it about candidates with the initials RP?), went on Colbert, he rose 2 percent in the Republican primary polls.

James H. Fowler, a professor of political science at the University of California–San Diego, found in a study that Democrats who appear on *The Colbert Report* enjoy a significant increase in the number and total amount of donations they receive in the next thirty to forty days, compared with similar candidates who do not appear on the show. There's a reason *Time* magazine named Stephen one of the 100 most influential people in the world.

What advice would I give candidates coming on late-night shows? Here are the rules to follow and, of course, if this works, I expect to be appointed ambassador to the Bahamas.

1. Think warming up for tennis, and volley back-and-forth.
2. Do your pre-interview and find out what they want to talk about.
3. It's like a debate. Do a quip and a short real answer to get out your message.
4. Work with the host and *do* something other than talk. This is where Jimmy Fallon's show gets it.
5. Don't talk polspeak. No one outside the Beltway knows what "bracket creep" is.
6. Watch the show beforehand, know the name of the bandleader, and when you walk out, acknowledge the audience and the band—you're not sitting down with Chuck Todd.
7. Listen to what the host says so you can react.
8. Make sure your fly is zippered.
9. Look like you are enjoying yourself.
10. And for God's sake, read *People* magazine and the sports page. There is a world outside the Beltway. It drives me nuts when I write speeches for politi-

cians and they ask, "Why did you mention LeBron James? Who is he?"

And the Eleventh Commandment: you are
    not funnier than the host, so don't try to
    outfunny him.

I like the fact that Jimmy Fallon does sketches, such as having the president slow-jam with him. Or a recent bit he did with Sarah Palin, something that was very funny and smart of her to do. Jimmy dressed as Vladimir Putin wearing a wig and a Russian suit, and made a call to Sarah Palin.

FALLON: Hello, Miss Palin, it's me, Vladimir.
PALIN: Vladimir? What are you doing calling me?

After Fallon/Putin asked if it's true she predicted a Russian invasion of the Ukraine back in 2008, she said, "You betcha, Vlad."

The bit went on with Jimmy saying he could have used her "predicting powers" in his "office March Madness pool," and she did this joke: "Bracket's good. You know, he's going to be six this month. Yeah. And Bracket just went out with Track and Jacket, and he shot his first bear."

At the end of the bit, Fallon/Putin said he needs to hang up so he can pick up vodka, and then says he wishes he had a neighbor who could pick some up for him. Palin said, "Alaska's not that far from Russia. Hold on a second."

Brilliant of Palin. Self-deprecating and likable.

The wild card in the political late night in the future will be Stephen Colbert. Take the influence of the Colbert Bump described above and double or triple his viewership on CBS at 11:35 at night. He could be a huge kingmaker. Bigger than the Koch brothers and George Soros, without spending billions. There is a reason that President Obama went on Colbert during Stephen's final few weeks. After a disastrous midterm the president was starting to make a comeback (Cuba, immigration, good economic numbers), so what better place than a late-night show to add a little wind beneath the approval-rating wings.

With the Colbert new show debut, even with Jay and Dave off the air, the importance of late night will continue to grow.

When we look back at the history of politicians on late night I suspect more than anything that we'll recall the "recall," when Arnold came on *The Tonight Show with Jay Leno* and announced he was running for governor.

CHAPTER SEVEN

Arnold

WHEN NEWS REALLY DOES
HAPPEN ON LATE NIGHT

Just as people say they were there, as in, "I was there when Kobe scored 81," or "I was there when Janet Jackson's nipple popped out," I really was there the night of the Arnold announcement.

Over the years I had written jokes for Arnold when he did roasts, charity events, speeches, and talk-show appearances. That came about when Arnold was left to me in someone's will. Back in 1996, my agent told me I needed to learn to write a sitcom. He suggested I work with legendary sitcom writer Milt Rosen, who for $1,800 would take me through a ten-week course on how to write one. So I hired Milt, and every Thursday I would go over to his house, learn at the feet of Buddha, and work on a sitcom script, and the next week we would review it and go to the next step. Bottom line, he was a wonderful teacher, I learned how to write a sitcom, and ended up selling a few shows (*The Merchants of Venice Beach*, *The Puppet Show*, *K Street*).

A few years later, Milt was sick and didn't have long to go, and I would stop over at his house every once in a while, bring him matzah ball soup, and see how he was doing. He passed away in August 2000, and a few days later his widow called me. "Milt left you something," she said. Since he wasn't rich I was a little stunned. I said, "What did he leave me?" She said, "He left you Arnold Schwarzenegger."

Turns out that for years Milt had worked with Arnold, supplying him one-liners for special events at which Arnold would speak. As he was dying, he gave Arnold my number.

A few days later the phone rang and I heard a voice say, "I need chokes." Chokes? Wait, it's Arnold and he needs jokes. He was giving a toast at one of Tom Arnold's weddings or divorces, so I wrote some "chokes." Jokes sent, check arrived, a few days later another call came for another event. Arnold started hiring me on a regular basis.

So when he called me for jokes the day before his August 6, 2003, appearance on *The Tonight Show* as the governor's campaign was kicking off, I naturally asked, "Well, are you going to announce or not?" He said it was a surprise but that I should write the jokes under the assumption he wasn't going to run. That made sense to me. He was a friend of former LA mayor Richard Riordan. Riordan was a Republican who appealed to both parties, Gray Davis was so unpopular, and at the time of the recall, Arnold was still a very popular movie star and would be giving up about $150 million in *Terminator* movie money to run . . . so I was sure he was going to endorse Riordan.

As a general rule I didn't write for the guests on the show. They had their own material, or stories that they had reviewed with the producers. But sometimes the producers would ask the writers to help out the talent with a bit they wanted to do on the show and the writers would help; or there would be times when a friend of mine was coming on the show and if he or she called needing a few lines, I'd break out the laptop. It's all about making the best TV and making the guest feel comfortable.

So the night before the appearance I wrote Arnold about forty jokes, thirty-eight under the theory that he wasn't going to run, and two that he was. I often did that on news stories. When an O. J. Simpson or Robert Blake jury verdict was coming in I'd write ten to fifteen jokes both ways, guilty and not guilty, so that the second the verdict was announced, I could be the first one to hand them in to Jay. Yes, I'm that shallow . . . and competitive. Not all the jokes were political, but were the usual

Arnold: semi-risqué and funny. Above all, Arnold "gets" self-deprecating. The first joke I ever wrote for him was this:

> I AM LIVING PROOF that any immigrant can come to America and become a millionaire if he works hard, studies hard, and marries a Kennedy.

For some reason Republicans are much better at self-deprecation. Maybe because they believe they have God on their side. Which is the same thing ISIS says.

There were dozens of reporters set up on a stage next to our studio so that they could report what everyone was sure they knew—that Arnold wasn't going to announce. Before the show I did something I rarely do, which is go downstairs to meet the guest. The only guests I ever saw before the show were people I knew, like Billy Crystal, Robin Williams, President Obama, Joe Biden, Marty Short, Bob Costas, Hugh Jackman, Terry Bradshaw, Mary Matalin, Chris Rock, James Carville, and Arnold. Pretty diverse group. Another question I'm often asked is this: How do you write for different people? My daughter Sam pointed out to me that when I'm talking to Carville on the phone I always sound a little Cajun. Maybe it's a Zelig-like quality, where I imitate or emulate who I'm talking to, but it actually helps. Before I write for anyone, I like to listen to their voice on the phone for five minutes, just to literally get their voice and make me think like they do.

We went over his jokes and then I stayed in his dressing room with his publicist and George Gorton, a Republican consultant. We watched as Arnold and Jay did their segment, and then Jay asked him if it was a painful decision. Arnold delivered one of the jokes I had written that was in the "not running" pile. "It's the most difficult decision I've made in my entire life, except the one I made in 1978, when I decided to get a bikini wax."

At that point I *knew* he was never going to announce. What kind of person would make that joke and then announce he was running for one of the most important elected offices in the country? It was so clear he wasn't announcing that at one point Jay addressed the reporters offstage, saying they should have all been at Kobe's court hearing. Kobe was on trial then in Denver for a loose-ball foul.

Arnold and Jay continued the segment and then Arnold started talking about how Gray Davis had failed the state, and he went on and on about the kind of governor California needed—his preamble perfectly describing Dick Riordan. When he said, "And that is why" . . . I knew right there that Arnold would be saying, "And that is why I am endorsing Dick

Riordan for governor." Instead he took a stutter-step pause and said, "I am announcing for governor of Cal-ee-for-nia."

The place exploded. People started cheering and going nuts. Arnold's publicist, who was very pregnant at the time (not by Arnold), sank back in her chair. George Gorton turned the color of Edgar Winter (Google the name) and said, "Arnold is going to need a phone and a private room to call Maria."

It was suddenly clear to me, and to everyone else, that no one had known in advance, and Arnold had somehow in midsentence of his Riordan setup changed his mind.

Jay clearly didn't know, because he was for the first and maybe only time ever taken aback by something a guest said.

Then George Gorton said he needed a place to hold a press conference. Wouldn't you have had one lined up if your candidate was running? The show ended, and a late-night show probably elected an Austrian bodybuilder governor.

Not only that, Arnold became one of the greatest all-time sources for jokes. Here are a few from the night after he announced on our show:

> WE HAD A VERY EXCITING SHOW last night. How many watched the show last night? As you know, Arnold Schwarzenegger announced he's going to run for governor on our program last night. My

staff didn't know. His staff didn't know. I didn't know. I had all these questions about who he was going to support. If he doesn't get to be governor, maybe he should work for the CIA. He can keep a secret better than they can.

||||||||||

IF ARNOLD IS ELECTED, you know who I feel sorry for? The people on death row. Imagine you're about to be executed, the governor calls, you think it's a reprieve, you hear that "Hasta la vista, baby."

||||||||||

ARNOLD SCHWARZENEGGER says he expects his opponents to throw all kinds of dirt at him, and it started already. Today they released the one thing that could really hurt him—he once starred in a movie with Tom Arnold.

||||||||||

ARNOLD SCHWARZENEGGER has filed to run for governor. Gary Coleman has filed. Gallagher has filed. Larry Flynt . . . Angelyne . . . I don't know if it's an election or a bad episode of *Hollywood Squares*.

CHAPTER EIGHT

The Greatest Guests of All Time

Fred de Cordova started working in the Ziegfeld Follies in 1929, allegedly for seventy-two years never went a week without a show business paycheck, directed Jack Benny and George Burns and *My Three Sons* as well as *Bedtime for Bonzo*. For twenty years he was the executive producer for Johnny Carson, and after Jay took over, Fred stayed on as a consultant. Fred would come in every day for an hour or two, kibitz, watch the show, and drive home. As part of his deal, he was given free vodka and cigarettes. Once a week, a production assistant would go to Red Carpet Liquor in Glendale, buy him two cartons of Silva Thins and a couple fifths of vodka, and put them in the car.

I love show business. I wonder what the assistant would have done if Fred was addicted to hookers.

Fred was true old Hollywood, and by that I mean he smoked and drank nonstop. He died September 15, 2001, and gave rise to one of the sickest lines of all time: "Fred went out like the World Trade Center—bombed and smoking."

Okay, that was wrong. Too soon? I defer to the expertise of Chris Rock, who on *SNL* predicted that soon we'd be having 9/11 sales. Chris also said that he'd never visit the new Freedom Tower after 9/11:

> I AM NEVER going in the Freedom Tower. I don't care if Scarlett Johansson is butt-naked on the eighty-ninth floor, in a plate of ribs. I'm not going in there.

Fred de Cordova once told me that there were only twelve great talk-show guests at any given time. Of course, his idea of great guests included Francis X. Bushman and Tony Randall, but his point was that there are only a few guests who are truly entertaining. Guests with stories, who volley with the host, who aren't just there to plug their next project, who stay for the entire show to interact with guest number two.

Times have changed. Nowadays only the real pros like Billy

Crystal, Hugh Jackman, Tom Hanks, Marty Short, and Terry Bradshaw stay for the entire show and slide down the couch.

I don't get people who leave after their segment—you're a B-level actor and you are being seen by 4 million people and you can't spend an extra thirty minutes being witty? Where else are you going at four thirty in the afternoon when we tape?

Here are the greatest living late-night guests who make my hall of fame. The top thirty. They come prepared, interact, and enjoy being there. They are listed in alphabetical order because a lot of them are good friends and I don't want to elevate one over the other. To each of them I can say, you know I wanted to list you first.

Charles Barkley
Terry Bradshaw
Albert Brooks
Mel Brooks
Carol Burnett
George Clooney
Billy Crystal
Matt Damon
Michael Douglas
Will Ferrell
Tina Fey

Jamie Foxx

Arsenio Hall

Chelsea Handler

Tom Hanks

Neil Patrick Harris

Hugh Jackman

Norm Macdonald

Bill Maher

Steve Martin

Regis Philbin

Amy Poehler

Carl Reiner

Chris Rock

Charlie Sheen

Marty Short

David Steinberg

Wanda Sykes

Betty White

James Woods

Thanks to my *Tonight Show* "comma," I got to be friends with Terry Bradshaw. By comma I mean that which you are known for, which people always mention when introducing you, or which everyone thinks of when they see you. Example: Solange (all we can think of is, she kicked Jay Z in an elevator). Or, this is Jon Macks, *Tonight Show* writer and sports junkie. Back in 1999, Terry Bradshaw asked who on Jay's staff could write some sports jokes for him for a roast he was doing, and someone gave him my name. Since then we've become friends, and I have not only written a few lines here and there for Terry, but worked with him on his one-man show, which starred Terry and the greatest dance team I have ever seen, the I-Q-ties. Once, Terry and I were walking through the parking lot at NBC before the show when a crew member from another show walked up to Terry with a football and asked if he would throw him a pass. Now, Terry has a chronically bad shoulder and arm from all the passes he has thrown and the beatings they've taken over the years, but he obliged. The crew member ran about twenty yards and said, "Throw it." Terry said, "Go deep." Terry, as you may remember, never threw those dinky passes like the ones we see today, but always preferred to chuck it downfield. The crew member said something to the effect of "You're too old to throw it deep." It was like watching a Western in which the gunfighter shows the young punk how quick he really is. By the time the letter *p* crossed his lips in the word *deep*, Terry had his arm cocked and delivered a pass that traveled at Mach 2 to the crew member's chest. The crew member caught it and, with the air knocked out of him, managed to gasp "Thanks." Terry and I walked away. About ten seconds later he started to laugh, and said, "I can't move my arm."

As a general rule, comics are better than actors. Actors are used to playing someone else, so when they have to be themselves, as Gertrude Stein said about Oakland, there is no there there. Comics operate on their own personalities and opinions onstage, so they are, as a general rule, better guests, regardless of whose show they are on.

When Billy Crystal comes on a show, he is totally prepared. He has written some lines, he has some stories to tell, and he is there to entertain. If you have a chance, look up Billy's raccoon story from his appearance on Letterman in January 2009. Basically Billy was being tormented by a raccoon at his house, and for eight minutes plus, as he told the story, he had Dave and the audience in hysterics. It was absolute brilliance, and it worked because it was about something real, it featured Billy's personality, and it built and built until the end.

Another classic appearance was Marty Short on Conan O'Brien on May 1, 2014. Marty is another comic who is always, always, always prepared. It was right in the middle of the Donald Sterling craziness. Marty went in armed and he had Conan helpless with laughter. It's clear Conan is a big Marty fan and he is perfect in setting Marty up. Forget Stockton to Malone, O'Brien to Short is more impressive.

(Non–sports fans, Google Stockton to Malone.)

This was their back-and-forth:

MARTIN: You're so pale even Donald Sterling says "get some color."

CONAN: I have to ask you, what do you think of this whole Donald Sterling thing?

MARTIN: First of all, he's a good-looking kid and—

ANDY: I said on Twitter today he looks like Mike Wallace ate Mike Wallace.

MARTIN: It's frightening.

He's the only one who feels that *12 Years a Slave* is the feel-good movie of the year.

He watches it backward so it could have a happy ending.

He keeps looking at the screen.

They're getting away!

They're getting away!

He's a dreadful, dreadful, dreadful fella.

CONAN: He sure is.

MARTIN: I don't know why you hang with him.

What makes a guest great are the following: having something to talk about other than the project being plugged; the ability to back-and-forth with the host; the desire to be there, as opposed to acting as if the chance to promote some lame-ass movie like *The Canyons* is a gift you are bestowing on the world. Hey, it's a privilege to be in show business. As my friend Brad Lachman says, "Show business didn't choose you, you choose show business." If you don't like it, quit. Leave.

That's it. Be prepared, talk, and be happy. That's all it takes to be a great show business guest. And about twenty people can do it.

Ninety-five percent of the time celebrities come on shows to promote a movie, a TV show, or a new CD. Four percent of the time they come on because they are the world's greatest guests and a "friend of the show," which means the host loves them, they love the host, and they are incredibly entertaining.

There are some guests who are loyal to one show. I'm sure they were on Jay at some point, but I generally remember Bill Murray, Bruce Willis, and Will Ferrell always going on Dave. And Terry Bradshaw, Wanda Sykes, and Chelsea Handler always seemed to want to come on Jay. Did it make a lot of sense career-wise for some people to choose one host over the other? Not by the Nielsen ratings. But in terms of comfort level—absolutely.

For the math majors reading this, my above numbers added up to just 99 percent. Which brings me to the other 1 percent of the time a celebrity comes on a show—a mea culpa.

In 2014 Jonah Hill went on Fallon to apologize for using antigay slurs. Jonah said the wrong thing and then did the right thing. I don't believe for a second that Jonah Hill is a gay basher, so it was smart for him to go on and immediately use the forum of a late-night show, which is not a "gotcha" show, to make his case. You're Donald Sterling, you go on Anderson Cooper, you get crucified; you come on a late-night show and, well, in his case he still would get crucified. At the BET Awards Chris Rock said about Sterling, "He's an eighty-year-old white man. Did we need an Anderson Cooper investigation to find out he doesn't like black people?"

Hillary Clinton went on Jon Stewart after her comment that she and Bill were dead-broke after they left the White House. Smart of her to do so, and although her appearance didn't erase the comment, it allowed her to further explain what she meant.

Those are recent mea culpas. The most famous late-night mea culpa, which is Latin for "Boy, did I fuck up," occurred twenty years ago, in July 1995, when Hugh Grant came on *The Tonight Show*. Flash backward. Hugh Grant, one of the biggest movie stars in the world, is caught with a hooker named Divine Brown. He decides to come on our show, which for its first few years was losing to Dave in the ratings. Yes, we were inching closer and closer and winning once in a while, but Dave was the ratings champ.

Then Hugh Grant came on our show to talk about a mishap in which his penis accidentally got caught in a woman's mouth after he gave her $100. These things happen. Normally back then we had around five million people watch our show, but that night more than ten million watched.

It was July 10, 1995, and a miracle occurred. People who watched Jay and how he handled Hugh and the comedy on our show realized "This guy Leno is really good." They sampled our show for the first time in years and liked what they saw. Jay had changed from the first few years that he was host but no one knew he had grown. The set was different, he was closer to the audience, our comedy bits were more refined, and, best of all, the world's greatest monologuist was at the top of his game. And then Jay opened the segment with Hugh by doing what late-night shows do best—he spoke for all 300 million Americans when he asked Hugh a six-word question. "What the hell were you thinking?"

Ball game over. We started to win and remained the champ for the next nineteen years.

By the way, Hugh also handled himself well. He said, "I think you know in life what's a good thing to do and what's a bad thing, and I did a bad thing. . . . And there you have it."

Maybe Bill Cosby should have said the same thing. On his way to jail.

For Grant, it was a smart way to lance the boil, a boil he probably got from Miss Brown. Catholics have confession, Jews have Yom Kippur, celebrities have late night.

Sometimes it works, sometimes it doesn't.

A few years ago Kanye West embarrassed himself with Taylor Swift. At least the good news for Taylor is that he didn't marry her and then name their baby after two points on a compass. He interrupted her acceptance speech at the MTV Video Music Awards and then went on Jay to "explain." Now, sometimes an apology is in order. Other times America doesn't even need the apology, we just like to see the host make the guilty party squirm. Jay did that with one question: "What would your mother think?" Kanye looked like he was about to cry.

Judge Jay did what America wanted. Spoke for all of us and made a point. Kanye recovered and went on to become Yeezus and the third or fourth Mr. Kim Kardashian.

Eliot Spitzer also came on Jay for his mea culpa. Mr. "I won't wear a condom but I will wear my socks during sex" got caught diddling a hooker named Ashley Dupré. With a name like that, you just know she's a ten, and ten on the hot-crazy index. That's Sarah Palin territory.

Eliot came on, took his nationwide punishment, showed the world he was contrite and smart, and then went on to lose his election. So sometimes it doesn't always work. If there is a rule we can learn from Hugh Grant and Eliot Spitzer about confessing after being caught with a hooker, it's this: You have a better chance of surviving if you have sex in a car than doing it in a hotel and forgetting to take your socks off.

Or you can be like Charlie Sheen, a great guy and a great guest. Charlie never came on Jay to apologize about hookers, he *owned* it. What makes Charlie great is that he is willing to make fun of himself. He knows there's an elephant in the room and he's not afraid to point it out. One bit that comes to mind was where Jay "went" to his house. Charlie opened the door, and while they talked, there were cheerleaders parading behind him.

In Charlie's final appearance, Jay busted him about not only being one of our most frequent guests, but canceling the most times. Jay ad-libbed about Charlie's lack of creativity in coming up with excuses, saying, "Charlie, you had your wisdom teeth pulled four times."

Charlie's response: "I had sixteen wisdom teeth."

CHAPTER NINE

Joking About a Rumor and Twisting the Truth

HOW LATE NIGHT DEALS WITH MAKING FUN FACTS OUT OF UN-FACTS

Individual jokes can create news and cause public reaction. Back in 1973 Johnny Carson did a joke that caused a nation-wide toilet paper shortage. It started when a congressman said that a shortage of paper pulp meant that the General Services Administration was 50 percent short of its goal of ordering toilet paper. AP and a series of newspapers reported on it, but no big deal. Then, on December 19, 1973, Johnny announced in his monologue that there was a shortage of toilet paper. It was buttockal Armageddon. People rushed the stores, stores started stockpiling and rationing, they over-ordered, orders went unfilled, more panic set in, and price gouging began. Want to know how late night impacts us? For a month Americans had to clench and pray there'd be enough Charmin to clean out their butts, thanks to Johnny.

Another joke that had an impact beyond its telling was a joke Jay did. After it was announced in 2004 that Jay would go off the air in 2009 and be replaced by Conan, people began to speculate "What would Jay do next?" I wrote a joke one day about an earthquake we had. The premise was that experts say that during an earthquake you should always go somewhere big, safe, and secure. Jay said, "I'm heading over to ABC." It was a JOKE. I could have typed *Fox* instead of ABC. Jay might have decided not to do the joke. A day or so later, the trade newspapers started talking about how Jay might go to ABC. I think that's what started NBC to come up with their idea for the ten p.m. show. So if you didn't like that show, it's my fault.

By being willing to do a joke based on a rumor, late-night-show hosts can have an impact on pop culture. And when the jokes are told in monologues night after night, the rumor becomes fact. There's that great line from the movie *The Man Who Shot Liberty Valance*: "When the legend becomes fact, print the legend." With late night, when the rumor seems believable, joke about the rumor.

And sometimes late night just makes up something that becomes fact. Of all the jokes told and all the sketches performed on late night about politicians, none has had a "thermostat" impact like Tina Fey's portrayal of Sarah Palin. It defined Palin forever, and is a reference we'll never forget. We all remember Sarah saying, "I can see Russia from my house." There's only one problem. Sarah never said that, Tina Fey did.

What Sarah said in an interview with ABC's Charles Gibson was "They're our next-door neighbors, and you can actually see Russia from land here in Alaska, from an island in Alaska." That is, in fact, true. From Alaska's Little Diomede Island you can see Russia's Big Diomede Island.

This is what Tina did two days after the Palin-Gibson interview, on the 2008 season premiere of *Saturday Night Live*, in a sketch portraying Sarah Palin with Amy Poehler as Hillary Clinton:

FEY AS PALIN: You know, Hillary and I don't agree on everything. . . .

POEHLER AS CLINTON: Anything. I believe that diplomacy should be the cornerstone of any foreign policy.

FEY AS PALIN: And I can see Russia from my house.

Now, I don't think anyone was ever going to confuse Sarah Palin's intellect for that of Margaret Thatcher or Madame Curie (people under fifty, please Google). But after Tina Fey's performances, what Sarah said didn't matter. The joke became real. Once again, "When the legend becomes fact, print the legend."

It's similar to everyone believing Al Gore said he invented the Internet. He never said that. What he said was this: "During my service in the United States Congress I took the initiative in creating the Internet. I took the initiative in moving forward a whole range of initiatives that have proven to be important to our country's economic growth and environmental protection, improvements in our educational system."

In other words, Gore claimed credit for votes he had made while in Congress to expand and enable the Internet.

That didn't matter.

> You guys heard about Al Gore and Tipper splitting up? Everybody is talking about it. Everyone's blogging about this, and now there are reports online that his daughter and her husband are splitting up. I bet this is the one week where Al Gore wishes he didn't invent the Internet.
>
> —JIMMY FALLON

There is a new bill in the Senate that is upsetting a lot of people. This bill would give the president the power to shut off the Internet. Al Gore is strongly opposed to it. Not because he invented the Internet. Because he did. But because he just signed up for Match.com.

—CRAIG FERGUSON

And Letterman had a great list:

TOP TEN OTHER ACHIEVEMENTS CLAIMED BY AL GORE

10. Was first human to grow an opposable thumb.
9. Only man in world to sleep with someone named "Tipper."
8. Current vice president—Moesha fan club.
7. He invented the dog.
6. While riding his bicycle one day, accidentally invented the orgasm.
5. Pulled the US out of early '90s recession by personally buying 6,000 T-shirts.
4. Starred in CBS situation comedy with Juan Valdez, *Juan for Al, Al for Juan.*

3. Was inspiration for Ozzy Osbourne song "Crazy Train."

2. Came up with popular catchphrase "Don't go there, girlfriend."

1. Gave mankind fire.

Look at number 7—late night had so painted the picture of Al Gore's saying that he invented the Internet that a joke about his inventing something else was instantly believable. The unspoken setup was what he had never really said.

Boom, the jokes were so entrenched in popular culture and so widespread and believable that even Bill Clinton made an Al Gore joke during one of his Gridiron speeches:

> AL GORE INVENTED the Internet. For the record, I, too, am an inventor. I invented George Stephanopoulos.

The reason that joke and the concept are believable is because late-night hosts had spent years and years delivering jokes painting Gore as a boring, pompous blowhard. He was *South Park*'s ManBearPig and a loser. Leno did a joke I loved:

TIME MAGAZINE has named everyone their "Person of the Year." And somehow, Al Gore still came in second.

So what is the effect of those years and years of Gore jokes? Are jokes like that the reason why Al didn't win the presidency? No, he didn't win because he lost his own home state of Tennessee and ran away from a popular president who gave us a great economy with ten million new jobs. (Right now, how many people would be happy to have 5 percent unemployment and a president getting daily head? I would.) So did the jokes result in Bush winning? No . . . but the jokes sure didn't help Gore. Forget the dangling chads, maybe a few hundred people, after listening to all those jokes over the years, decided they didn't want a cadaver for president. If I sound like I'm mad at Al Gore, I am. A better campaign and he's president and we never end up invading Iraq. I don't care if he solves climate change, he owes the world a daily apology for bungling his campaign.

Saturday Night Live has a special place in defining the way we look at our candidates. From Fey's Palin to Chevy Chase's clumsy Gerald Ford to Dana Carvey's 41, *SNL* can paint that canvas. Think about it—did people learn about President George H. W. Bush's points of light from the White House or from Dana Carvey? If you said anything but "Dana," it "wouldn't be prudent."

There are harmless rumors late-night hosts joke about: Madonna is dating a twenty-five-year-old—maybe she is, maybe she isn't, he could be twenty-five, who cares if some young man likes to collect antiques. And then there are ones that do matter, i.e., in the middle of a presidential campaign it's rumored that John Edwards is having an affair. I don't think there are any hard-and-fast rules about it, but the cheat that writers use to get the joke in the monologue is "it's been reported." So let's say as we go through our daily websites, newspapers, and tabloids that we see that the *National Enquirer* says that famous actor Joe Doakes is a drunk. Jay would say something like "The *National Enquirer* reports—and you know how they check, recheck, and recheck their facts—that Joe Doakes is a drunk." That fact is true—it was reported—and that fulfills a rule of topical late-night monologues—the setup is true or is reported as true, and then comes the joke.

Probably the most famous example of that was the Lewinsky cigar story. When Matt Drudge broke the "rumor" in August of that year that a sexual act had occurred between the president and an intern involving a cigar, the mainstream media refused to report it. But as the *American Journalism Review* notes,

"Members of the public who watch late-night monologues or listen to morning shock jocks knew about the cigar for some time."

Then, a few weeks later when the Starr report came out, the world learned that the salacious rumor Drudge had reported was in fact true. Everyone was reporting about it and talking about it; it even made the Emmys that year when Chris Rock came out with a cigar and said, "Early on in comedy this was used as a prop, and today it still is."

Since then or perhaps because of the *Drudge Report* and late-night comics, the mainstream media has been far more adventurous in how they share information. They have a clever way of reporting the rumors that have been turned into jokes on late night. Their favorite is to have a panel discuss whether it is appropriate for them to report that Joe Doakes has a drinking problem. After a thirty-minute discussion by a team of non-experts (FYI: very few of the political experts you see on TV have ever run a campaign—the key is, if they're attractive, they are not real political consultants; real political consultants have bad hair, if they have any at all, and muffin middles; Donna Brazile said that you're not a political strategist just because you voted once), they come to the conclusion that it's not appropriate for them to report on the drunken Doakes *despite* the fact that for the previous thirty minutes that's all they talked about. The other way is to show the jokes of the late-night hosts on their newscasts, thus broaching the topic, and then tsk-tsk that those wild and crazy hosts have gone too far. The result: the late-night hosts have in fact broken the news.

Mike Murphy has a shrewd take on it. Two things to know about Mike. One, he is a great dinner companion, a political genius, and a legendary Republican consultant. And, two, he is such a good guy that when I asked him to jot down his thoughts so that I could include them, he was polite enough not to say, "But, Jon, you're just trying to get me to do your job." Here are Mike's observations:

> LATE NIGHT has become important in politics because it is both widely viewed and very topical. It is the most important place where pop culture intersects with political happenings in front of a large audience. Regular entertainment programming might make the odd reference to politics on occasion and TV news is always up to the minute, but only late night on the networks and the "fake news" shows on Comedy Central combine the two in front of a big audience. When something sticks— a catchphrase, a powerful joke, a funny interview moment or gaffe—it sticks for days and becomes a very big

moment. The late shows grab the moment and run with it for days, and then the straight-news shows pick it up and report on it as a political development. Suddenly the whole campaign is about that moment, often for weeks or even longer. It can be good, it can be very bad, but either way the power of the late-night shows has become an important factor in American politics.

There was an axiom in American life that a man is innocent until proven guilty. I use the word *was* because it's no longer true. In 2015 a person can be indicted by Nancy Grace and then tried and found guilty by the court of late-night TV. Even if an actual court later finds him innocent, we the people have, thanks to late night, judged him guilty as charged. And that's because despite what a jury may find, we with common sense and in the joke world know who is really guilty. As I once wrote about O.J.—the prosecutors are trying to railroad a guilty man.

O.J.—Guilty.
Robert Blake—Guilty.
Richard Jewell—Uh-oh.

That last one was bad. Sometimes the rumor isn't true and lives are damaged. There were two times I felt really bad. Richard Jewell and Senator Bob Menendez.

Everyone just knew Richard Jewell was the Atlanta Olympic bomber. Of course he was guilty—he was fat and dumb looking. If Flounder from *Animal House* had put on 100 pounds and been dumber, he would have been Richard Jewell. Late-night hosts found him an easy target. Only one problem. He was 100 percent innocent. The problem was he was just a regular guy doing his job and he was unfairly blamed. To this day I'm haunted by the jokes I wrote. He was innocent, the jokes were mean, and I'm pretty sure they were mine.

I learned my lesson from that, and for years I was very careful before writing a joke about someone who was being damned by unproved rumors. Not that this is an excuse (okay, it is), but late-night hosts were just following the lead on Jewell from the news reports that had pegged him as the number-one suspect. In this case, we were both thermometer and thermostat.

So I was good and careful until 2013, when I saw a story that alleged that New Jersey US senator Bob Menendez had been involved with some hookers from the Dominican Republic. Bingo. Off to the races. The fact that there was an FBI linkage and that it was true he was being investigated made it easy. I could set up the joke by saying it was reported that the FBI was investigating Senator Bob Menendez.

> THE FBI is investigating New Jersey Senator Bob Menendez for allegedly soliciting Dominican prostitutes. So, once again, foreign workers are doing the jobs Americans don't want to do.
>
> The FBI says Menendez agreed to pay the prostitutes $500, but then only gave them $100. So, he had sex like a Democrat but is a fiscal conservative like Republicans. That's what we need in Washington! We need more men like that! Yeah. A little different when they're spending their own money, huh?

The Tonight Show was the first on a major network to bring up the scandal, with the exception of CNBC's Larry Kudlow and the Fox News Channel.

A few months later the story fizzled out, and it turns out he didn't hire cheap hookers. I felt a little guilty about that, although not at the Richard Jewell level of atonement, because (1) Menendez is a senator and a big boy, and (2) as a taxpayer he works for me, so technically he can't be mad at his boss.

But that is an example of how late-night hosts can give a person what I call "the comma."

THE COMMA

You can't un-ring a bell. And you can't ever disassociate yourself from the descriptive word that follows the comma after your name.

There's an old joke about Giuseppe. Giuseppe is drinking in a bar and he's very depressed. The bartender asks him what the matter is. Giuseppe says, "I helped build the Brooklyn Bridge. Do they look at me and say, there goes Giuseppe, the bridge builder? No. When I was a lifeguard, I saved a hundred people from drowning. Do they say, there goes Giuseppe, the lifesaver? No. But you suck just one cock. . . ."

That's Giuseppe's comma. Here are some of the people with commas affixed to their names, due in large part to the way our perceptions have been shaped about them through late-night jokes. In some of the cases the comma fits; in others, not so much.

Al Gore, boring.
Gerald Ford, clumsy.
Gary Busey, insane.
Paula Abdul, airhead.
Dan Quayle, dumb.

Patsy Ramsey, guilty.

Lindsay Lohan, drunken strumpet.

Christine O' Donnell, witch.

Do you remember Christine? US Senate candidate in 2010. She was a virgin, which will not cost you the election, and she practiced witchcraft, which generally will hurt you, unless you are running in LA. This was a year when Democrats were a disaster and it looked like she had a chance. Then Bill Maher aired a clip of her on his old show *Politically Incorrect*, in which she admitted that she used to dabble in witchcraft. The jokes began and didn't let up, and reached a level that made her feel compelled to produce and air a TV ad of herself saying, "I am not a witch."

Christine O'Donnell lost her election by 20 percent. In a brief concession speech, she said, "I'm melting."

—CRAIG FERGUSON

Christine O'Donnell released a commercial in which she says, "I'm not a witch." That's pretty good, though not as effective as her opponent's slogan, "I'm not Christine O'Donnell."

—JIMMY FALLON

Today we found out that a third college Christine
O'Donnell said she attended has no record of ever
knowing her. I'm starting to wonder if she ever
really went to Hogwarts.

—BILL MAHER

And then she said she was anti-masturbation. Bingo! Jay said:

IN THE DELAWARE Republican US Senate primary, the Tea Party candidate—a woman named
Christine O'Donnell—won a huge upset. Interesting woman. Very conservative. And she has come
out against masturbation. So not only is she against
politicians putting their hands in our pockets, she's
against you putting your hands in your own pockets
as well.

We even combined the two topics:

MORE PROBLEMS for candidate O'Donnell. It seems
she canceled all her Sunday talk-show appearances
after a video surfaced of her on Bill Maher's TV
show where she admitted she once dabbled in witch-

craft. So apparently, she is pro-dabbling but anti-diddling.

Would she have won without this? Maybe. But once she became the punch line, ball game over. Two years later, Bill Maher had her on his show and said to her, "I made your life hell and I'm sorry about that." He said that he didn't mean for the clips of her on *Politically Incorrect* to be such a big factor in her Senate race. Too late.

Donald Trump has his own special comma. Not only is his name a punch line, he may be one of the few people who, if you just see his photo, makes you immediately leap to this word: *assclown*.

Marty Short has a great joke: "What is it about *redheads* on television that make us laugh so much? Carol, Lucille Ball, Donald Trump."

Why do late-night shows like Jay, Dave, Jimmy, and Conan tend to focus on the sex lives of politicians rather than on bigger issues such as the national debt? It's because we all have sex unless we are Tim Tebow, Lolo Jones, or a pre–wedding night Jana Duggar. Jay told me that when you do a joke about Iran-Contra and guns and hostages and Sandinistas, people's eyes glaze over. We don't know anyone who is an arms trader. But we all know someone who has had an affair.

Jay, Dave, Jimmy K., and Conan go for fast, tighter jokes in a monologue.

The Stewarts and Colberts and Olivers can do (and do it great) the longer, complicated-issues jokes. In June 2014, John Oliver may have given Dr. Oz his permanent "comma." In this case, in June 2014 John took on Dr. Oz. You know the beloved Dr. Oz, the one who hawks more ridiculous supplements than Lance Armstrong. There's even something called the "Dr. Oz effect," by which his blessing of neti pots and the like can change the beliefs of millions of hapless stay-at-home moms who are fresh off refusing to get their kids vaccinated based on the scientific research and genius of Dr. Jenny McCarthy.

Dr. Oz had just finished testifying before a Senate subcommittee investigating the marketing of weight-loss scams, some of which Oz featured on his show. But who cares about a Senate hearing? Then John Oliver took him on, and in a brilliant sixteen-minute segment destroyed Oz's shameless pandering. (Oliver also has the time in his cable format to spend sixteen minutes on one topic.) Oz had bragged about the fat-fighting benefits of various dietary supplements on his own show, using phrases like "miracle in a bottle" and "lightning in a bottle" to describe unproved products. He's a doctor, so he wields influence and radiates credibility even when he's exaggerating out his ass.

John said, "What's so wrong with that? Name me one case where a man named Oz claimed mystical powers and led people astray."

He then pointed out that despite denying he did this in front of the Senate, Oz endorsed green coffee bean extract—a compound that may actually be harmful—as "magic beans" on his show. So, Dr. Oz, you were taken down by late night. Maybe he recovers, maybe he doesn't. But if John Oliver convinced one person to stop buying the crap Oz promotes, late night has done a great service.

The most famous comma of all time was a celebrity comma:

RICHARD GERE, gerbil up the ass.

Poor Richard Gere. It was actually just watercooler gossip and not late-night comics who gave him his comma. There were very few actual late-night jokes, although I do remember one from Craig Ferguson:

IN THE MOVIES, the chipmunks always break into song. So when I see a chipmunk in real life I wonder

if it can sing. Just like when I see a gerbil, I wonder
if it knows Richard Gere.

We all know that there is no way Richard Gere actually had
a gerbil up his ass. Trust me, I've tried it and they don't fit.
Great, now I have another comma.

CHAPTER TEN

The Juice Is Loose

Rumors can become accepted truth. And late-night hosts can use their power of hearsay and common sense to get to the truth. John Oliver's Dr. Oz takedown illustrated the common sense. But this kind of story is best found in the case of one Orenthal James Simpson.

O.J. was, is, and will always be one of the biggest stories late-night shows joked about. And that is where I feel all the shows did their job, convicting a guilty man that a jury found innocent.

For those who don't remember, with O.J. you had the tragedy of two innocent people killed by a team of Colombian drug lords . . . wait . . . by an unknown assailant. Okay, we all knew it was O.J.

But how do you joke about two people being brutally murdered? The key again was to find things about the trial that were stupid without addressing the murders.

And did that trial provide plenty: Kato Kaelin, Judge Ito, the sexual tension between Marcia Clark and Christopher Darden, the fighting lawyers, the Bruno Magli shoes, and of course the glove that did not fit.

FEUDING O. J. SIMPSON attorneys F. Lee Bailey and Robert Shapiro finally buried the hatchet. They buried it right next to the knife.

|||||||||||

JOHNNIE COCHRAN is such a good lawyer, even O.J. thinks he's innocent.

|||||||||||

THERE'S A NEW O.J. watch. It works fine, except there's an hour missing from ten to eleven.

Two weeks after the murders, a spokesman for *The Late Show* said that no one should expect David Letterman to joke about

O.J. because of the sensitivity of the issue. Maybe we felt differently because it was LA-based, but it became a staple of our monologue for several years. O.J. jokes made a comeback more than a decade later when he was finally convicted of stealing back his own memorabilia, and then he made even another return to monologues when he put on sixty pounds in prison. In fact, he made it into a *Tonight Show* joke run: "O.J. is so fat, he's changed his name from O.J. to *Au Jus.*" "O.J. is so fat, he wants the judge to throw the cookbook at him." And my favorite joke in that run was "O.J. is so fat that a prison movie about him will be called *The Veal Shank Redemption.*"

Now, how do "fat jokes" jibe with my key to comedy? Make fun of what people do, not who they are. Like all rules, there are exceptions. And when you are a robbing double murderer, we can make fun of EVERYTHING about you.

The O.J. jokes in 1994 and 1995 laid the groundwork for Jay as the late-night leader. He got there, as they say in military strategy school, "the firstest with the mostest," and in so doing, owned the story. Where Dave's great strength can be centered around himself (his "feuds" with Cher and Oprah), Jay's strength is to own a topic. We were the first to tackle the topic, we found a way to do it cleverly, we never did jokes about the tragedy, and we had a clear point of view: that a media circus and dumb jurors are missing the point that O.J. did it.

The critics didn't like the fact that we were focused on this topic. These would be the critics who were paid by newspapers that featured coverage of the trial every day on their front pages. The hypocrisy of those who are in that role is amazing. As my buddy James Carville once said about a newspaper criticizing the campaign donors of one of his candidates, "I will never take lessons in morality from people who make money selling ads for liquor, tobacco, and erectile dysfunction drugs."

The trial was twenty years ago, and Jay did an O.J. joke in 2013. And got criticized for it. The reason we did the joke was because O.J. was in the news again due to a parole hearing, and the story was everywhere. So if you're upset that he's in the news again, complain to CNN, not me. We're not pulling O.J. out of our ass, which is what his cell mate might be doing. We as comedy writers are reading sources and writing jokes about what you are watching and reading.

Sorry, had to get that one off my chest.

Despite the Letterman show's publicist saying Dave would not joke about O.J., soon Letterman jumped on the bandwagon. And scored. I remember this as one of his earlier jokes:

JURY SELECTION is continuing for the O.J. trial. They're looking for people who live in the Los Angeles area who are able to take six months out of their lives and who don't read the paper or watch the news. Can I suggest Ronald Reagan?

And then, just as happened later with September 11, with each passing day, the jokes became sharper. It's said that tragedy plus time equals comedy (unless it's a joke about Abe Lincoln). As the great Mel Brooks said, "I cut my finger. That's tragedy. A man walks into an open sewer and dies. That's comedy."

Either way, the clowns in that trial were ripe for ridicule. Again, it was left to late-night shows to do what they do best and what Americans love—making fun of those in charge. O.J. was probably the first convergence of twenty-four-hour news cycles, a major trial that was serious, and late night shining the spotlight on the fact that we are obsessed with celebrity. This didn't happen with Charlie Manson or the Nuremberg trials. Although all the late-night shows would have had a field day with Goering.

And the truth is, we learned so much from late night's take on the O.J. trial. Like the fact that there's a double standard when it comes to celebrities, that a key part of being a defense lawyer is knowing how to rhyme, and that jurors get conjugal visits. Wow, nine dollars a day plus nookie, can't beat it. Plus, in the end, the trial of the century gave us Dancing Itos and a parody of *Gilligan's Island* that used the words "a millionaire and a knife" instead of "a millionaire and his wife." The critics may not have liked it but people who watched the show did.

CHAPTER ELEVEN

Handling Sensitive Subjects

On *The Tonight Show* the monologue would sometimes get cut after the taping. Jay might have a thirty-joke monologue he would do on the show before the audience, but if a guest went a little long or if the monologue seemed a bit long, a few jokes would be cut before the show was broadcast. If they hadn't lost their topicality, they would be done the next night. As a general rule, the jokes that got cut were right at the end, so we would end on a video "drop-in" or, once in a while, lift a few in the middle that could be taken out easily. I, however, made history. In 4,610 shows only one opening joke was ever cut for being maybe too sensitive, and it was mine.

YOU KNOW THAT crazy pastor down there in Florida that was going to have the Koran burning? You
know that story, right? Well, he canceled it. He will
not be burning the Koran. In fact, today when President Obama heard that, he said, "Praise Allah."

Jay loved the joke but there was discussion among the producers
whether it was fair. Now, other shows had done Muslim Obama
jokes before, and we certainly had no problem doing this joke
about the president's alleged background: "These White House
scandals are not going away anytime soon. . . . People in Kenya
are now saying he's 100 percent American. That's how bad it's
gotten."

Anyway, when Jay did the joke, it got that great reaction I
love—laughs, "ohhs," and nervous looks. And after the taping,
the joke was cut, as it just wasn't the right thing to do.

And Allah knows I'm not the type to do a cartoon drawing
of the prophet Muhammad . . . but only because I can't draw.
But if I could I would do it today. Je Suis Charlie. But what
about sensitive subjects? There's a legendary joke by Johnny
Carson that says it all:

LINCOLN'S BIRTHDAY reminds me of my old girlfriend back in Nebraska. Gina Statutory. Her name

was Gina Statutory. She went to Lincoln High and she was voted Miss Lincoln, because every guy in school took a shot at her in the balcony.

When the joke didn't work, Johnny added, "Too soon." A hundred years after Lincoln died and it was still too soon.

Perhaps the most famous example of "too soon" is Gilbert Gottfried. I was working with Gilbert at *Hollywood Squares* and he was doing the Hugh Hefner roast in November 2001. We were backstage working on lines he would do that day on *Squares* and he mentioned that he wanted to run a joke by me that he was going to do at the Hefner roast: "I have to leave early tonight, I have to fly out to LA. I couldn't get a direct flight, I have to make a stop at the Empire State Building."

I love Gilbert. I love his comedy. I told him not to do it. Telling any comic not to do a joke is like telling a Kardashian not to sleep with a rapper. (At the 2014 BET Awards, the producers told Chris Rock not to do a joke that would embarrass a performer before introducing him. So Chris said, "Our next performer just signed a big deal; unfortunately, it's a plea deal. Please welcome Chris Brown.") So, despite the warning, Gilbert went to the roast and did the joke. It bombed. There were crickets. "Crickets" are how we describe a joke when it gets negative laughter—silence in the room.

And then Gilbert did the greatest saver of all time. A saver is a joke that is told after another joke bombs. Carson would always use a line like "May the Great Camel of Giza leave you a present in your undershorts." Legend has it that savers were invented by a head writer of Johnny's named Marshall Brickman.

Gilbert's saver was to tell the Aristocrats joke, a filthy jazz improv–like story that every comic has told in some form. Gilbert's save has become so legendary in comedy circles that a movie was made about it.

To his credit, and on at least one occasion the result was his getting fired, Bill Maher may be the only late-night comic who never worries about "too soon." But for the most part late-night comics have to feel their way around those big events that dominate the news. We do topical monologues, and when the news is dominated for weeks at a time by one story, how do we handle it? There was 9/11; the fact that two people were dead in the O.J. case; the shuttle explosions; Timothy McVeigh; the Boston Marathon bombings; Benghazi, Ferguson, Eric Garner—these are big, tragic stories. And our job is to somehow find the funny in the tangential events around the main story or the oddities connected with it. So for a story like Benghazi:

A CHICAGO MAN set a new world record for riding a Ferris wheel: "The only way to go around and around the circle that many times is to read the official report on Benghazi."

|||||||||||

THE PRESIDENT SAID he didn't know about the IRS scandal: "He was too busy not knowing anything about Benghazi to not know anything about" the IRS.

Notice how the way to get into one subject is to tie it to another. Of course, if I had thought of it, we would have had the Dancing Gaddafis to join our Dancing Itos. By doing this and telling association jokes or tangential jokes, late night allows us to deal with the fact that every day there are tragedies in the news. It's how we recognize that there is an elephant in the room.

The question really goes back to Carson's line—when is it really too soon? It was a question we all wrestled with in the days after September 11. I remember sitting around the office as we talked about what day we would go back on the air. Jay wanted to wait until after Dave came back on the air. I wasn't in the room or reading Jay's thoughts but my sense is Jay felt it should be Dave, as someone in New York, who should set the tone and speak first on behalf of the city. And to his credit, Letterman was perfect. His first show back was September 17,

2001. His guests were Dan Rather, who set the tone, and Regis, for comfort. Dave's monologue really captured what we were all feeling.

> AS I UNDERSTAND IT, another, smaller group of people stole some airplanes and crashed them into buildings. And we're told that they were zealots, fueled by religious fervor . . . religious fervor. And if you live to be a thousand years old, will that make any sense to you? Will that make any goddamned sense?

So now that Dave was back on, it was our turn. The time came to get ready for our first show, and we and all the late-night shows were in a dilemma. As human beings, our hearts ached for our brothers and sisters back east. As comedy writers, we made a series of sick jokes among ourselves to relieve the tension. And as professionals we had an acceptable monologue to write.

Our show opened with an American flag and without the usual upbeat musical opening. Our guests were Senator John McCain and the musical group Crosby, Stills and Nash, and then Jay organized an auction for a Harley-Davidson motorcycle signed by celebrities with the money going to 9/11 support organizations. In the monologue, after paying tribute to the heroes and those who lost their lives, Jay, as he often did in these situations, raised the question whether a show that regularly poked fun at the government could continue to do so after the attacks. Then he made the point that our job was to make people laugh and that our one hour a night might be a welcome break from the bad news of the day.

Here is his monologue from that night:

TUESDAY, SEPTEMBER 18, 2001

LET ME TELL YOU why we're back tonight. As you know, it was one week ago today, and this is our first show back. Well, we're back because the president of the United States, the mayor of New York, have asked us to try and get back into some sort of routine. Get back into what we normally do. Those of you watching at home, if you don't know this, we do not do our show in New York. We are in Los Angeles. Although we've seen all these horrible, horrible images on TV, I can't imagine how horrible they must be in person. And for that reason our prayers go out of course to the victims, the victims' families, the incredibly brave men and women of the New York Police and Fire Department. To see

300 people literally march into a building with not much chance of coming out to save people they've never even met. To see average Americans—just anybody here fighting with terrorists on an airplane to protect that airplane from crashing into the Capitol of the United States. You know, we hear so much about the greatest generation, and these people are certainly the greatest people of our generation. It's just an amazing, amazing story. It's amazing what a small, small country this is when we think of others instead of ourselves.

I'll tell you a story—when I first came out here to LA, and you know I used to tease my mother about this. I used to think this was so funny. I'd be here in Los Angeles, my mom was in Boston, and something would happen in San Francisco, there would be a train wreck, there would be a fire in Seattle, a bus would turn over in Vancouver, and an hour later I'd get a phone call: "Are you okay? Is that near you?" I'd go, "Ma, it's like eight hundred miles away." I used to think, *What's the matter with her? What is that?* And yet this past week I find myself calling people in Schenectady, New York. Calling people in Buffalo. Calling people in my hometown of Andover, Massachusetts. "Are you okay? Did a piece of that plane hit anybody?" You know, just that caring you have, that thinking of other people. And of course back to the original question, why are we here? You know, in a world where people fly airplanes into buildings for the sole purpose of killing innocent people, a job like this seems incredibly irrelevant. You know, normally I would be out here making fun of Democrats, making fun of Republicans.

And you realize we don't have Democrats or Republicans anymore, we only have Americans. We have Americans united in one goal for one reason. You know, it's hard to believe nine days ago the biggest story in the United States was the *Barbara Walters Special*. The cover of the magazine—"Anne Heche is crazy." That was our biggest problem nine days ago. You know, you go, "Wow—was it really that innocent a time?"

Just nine days ago? But you know we still have a job to do. And I don't pretend that this is an important job. You know what this job is? This job is like a cookie to those firemen. That's what we do. We're standing there with a cookie, we're standing there with a glass of lemonade. When those people get home after a hard day. We're not trying to make anybody forget, we're just trying to take their mind off it for a minute. You know, you watch this horrible carnage on television and, I don't know, maybe a silly joke can help. Maybe something a little funny can help. In the coming weeks and months, we are not going to be inappropriate, we are not going to be insensitive, we're not going to do jokes about people of different color or who look different, or people's religion, because that is obviously not the American way and that is what they would want us to do.

I'll tell you a story—I was a Boy Scout when I was a kid. I was a terrible Scout. I wasn't a very good Scout. I'm kind of dyslexic. If you've ever seen the monologue, you've probably figured that out. I'd make a sheepshank and I'd make the knot and it wouldn't pull through. But I had pretty good teachers, and my scoutmaster was a pretty good guy. He believed that every kid should get something. So at the end of the year when we'd have the Scout banquet, you know when they were handing out that corny merit badge, and the electricity merit badge.

At the end of the thing he'd call me up and go, "All right, Leno, your job is, you are going to be the troop cheermaster. Your job when you see another Scout that's a little depressed or a little upset, your job is to go over and tell that Scout a joke or entertain him." I thought, *Boy, that's a pretty good job*. And I loved doing that job. And, you know, through some bizarre twist of fate, it pays a lot better now than it did then. You know something? It's basically the same job. And like I say, I don't pretend it's an important job, but we all can't be at the epicenter, we all can't be digging through the rubble. Because we're not there, but we can give blood, or we can tell jokes, or we can wash dishes, we can make sandwiches— there's stuff that we can do. President Bush has told us to go back to work. Try to get back to our lives. And this is what we're trying to do here.

You know, I mentioned my dad once before he passed away and I haven't mentioned him since. You know my dad used to be a prizefighter, and he used to say, "Fight the good fight." And that's what this is, folks. This is the good fight. There are no ifs, ands, or buts. This is not "Hey, maybe we did something." We didn't. We didn't. We got sucker-punched and we got knocked down, but when we get up, we will get up. So, in the days and weeks ahead, when you see us out here being silly and telling jokes, some people will understand and some won't. And those that don't, well *Nightline* is a great show, too. I like *Nightline*, and it's a great show, but sometimes when I watch it, *uhhh*. In times of crisis, I go there, but, boy, I go there every night, and as great as those guys are, I find myself, you think, I can't cry anymore, and then you see that pregnant mom, you see that father who lost his daughter, and it's just incredibly sad. So our job here, and your job, I think, is to keep fighting the good fight and God bless America.

Back in those dark and tragic days, our show was less of an attempt to convey the news in a funny way and more of a way to get everyone's minds off the news. So in the beginning the monologue's emphasis was on jokes that were based on studies, celebrity gossip, and what I call silly stories. Comedy writers call them "a man in Belgium."

For example: A man in Belgium is arrested after he is

caught having sex with a tree. This then gives us a chance to do a series of really stupid jokes about this somewhat odd and apparently European act of having sexual intercourse with bark. These are the silly, stupid jokes we do when this story crosses our desks:

> He was stumped.
> He got spruced up before sex.
> He pined for his tree.
> Like Republicans, he loves bush.

Now, those weren't the jokes we used, those are the type of jokes one can use. They're called "man in Belgium" because when Carson's monologue was light, they would tell the writers to make up stories about a man in Belgium. Nowadays, because of the Internet and access to stories around the world, there is no need to make up stories about the Belgians—after all, their proclivities for sex with trees are well documented. That is a joke. Please, let's not have the Flemish picketing my house.

Dave's monologue after 9/11 gave everyone "permission" to come back on the air. So the next night we were on, we cautiously looked for ways to tell actual jokes. On September 19 we did one joke that was a misdirection along with a few silly jokes. This was the opening few lines:

WE'RE BACK. We're going to try telling some jokes. Now, we're going to ease into this slowly, and as I said last night, be respectful. We'll try to take people's minds off of things for a little bit and have some fun. Because this is a tough time to do humor, this is not the only tough time. There's been other tough stretches in comedy. Remember, Kev, remember a couple of years ago when President Clinton stopped dating for a few weeks?

|||||||||||

THE NFL SAID TODAY they will resume playing professional football next week, which of course is bad news for the Cleveland Browns.

|||||||||||

I'M WATCHING TV today and I see one of these stupid radical fundamentalist attacking our country and he's blaming the world's problems on our Western ways and I said, "Uh, enough about Jerry Falwell."

That last one starts with misdirection and leads the audience in one direction with a punch line in the opposite direction. Thus the Falwell joke.

As the days went on, we looked for more and more ways to do jokes about the fact that there was one and only one story in the news. The key was to stay away from the tragedy and to look for ways to talk about the absurdity of our enemy. And just like the propaganda machines of the government in the First and Second world wars, late-night shows took up the role of demonizing our enemy.

After all, they were suicidal madmen hoping to end up with seventy-two virgins. Who wants a virgin, anyway? They don't know what they're doing, plus, what if the virgins were all Janet Reno and Condoleezza Rice?

Bin Laden was one of fifty-eight siblings. It's always the middle child who has problems.

We were being told that duct tape could stop an anthrax attack. This is not a good time to be the lead singer in the band Anthrax.

One of the first jokes Jay told was this:

IF YOU'RE PLANNING to fly and your name is Muhammad, your last name better be Ali.

The joke killed and that's because (1) we addressed our collective fear of flying, and (2) it was a smart way to mention Muhammad by referencing a beloved figure in Ali.

With each passing year, the jokes every comic told got sharper and a bit more cynical. As we got farther away from the event, there were new stories about the war and not about the actual 9/11 event: Saddam Hussein in a spider hole, his sons Uday and Qusay; incompetent shoe bombers; and finally the politicization of the wars, which meant that American senators and presidents were fair game. And as far as I am concerned, if you stop laughing at the idiots in Washington, it really does mean the terrorists have won.

Now that George Bush has captured Saddam Hussein, it raises the question, what's he going to get his dad for Christmas next year?

—JAY LENO

It was like Groundhog Day. He popped out of a hole, and we got four more years of Bush.

—BILL MAHER

President Bush says he doesn't want to use the capture of Saddam for political gain. He says he wants a very slow, public trial that would end about next November.

—JAY LENO

At the trial Saddam insisted he is still president, he is still in charge, despite the fact that his people disapprove of him and his top assistants are all in jail or going to jail. No, I'm sorry, that's President Bush.

—JAY LENO

How many folks were in Times Square for the New Year's Eve celebration? . . . Here in the United States they celebrate by dropping a ball off a roof. In Iraq they celebrate by dropping the dictator through the floor.

—DAVID LETTERMAN

Last week they gunned down Saddam Hussein's sons, Uday and Qusay, and they went through the villa where they found them and they were looking at the stuff that they left behind. And Uday, he had a briefcase, and it contained cheap vodka, underwear, cologne . . . and Viagra. Coincidentally, that's what President Bush found when he moved into the Oval Office.

—DAVID LETTERMAN

If you don't know anything about Uday and Qusay, these were bad guys. This is what they did all day: they watched pornos, they drank alcohol, and they gambled. Which of course has got Congress all worried because they're going, "They can shoot you for that?"

—JAY LENO

With the bodies of Qusay and Uday officially identified, attention turns now to the grieving process. . . . Qusay and Uday were beloved by hench-man and thug alike. Indeed, the entire goon community is in mourning. I think it's fair to say there will be many electrodes tonight that will be flying at half-testicle.

—SAMANTHA BEE

Saddam Hussein just gave himself up. I mean, hell, Michael Jackson put up more of a fight.

—DAVID LETTERMAN

On the Republican side, Rudolph Giuliani has dropped out. America's Mayor, John Q 9/11, it's over. For months, Giuliani was the front-runner for the

Republican nomination, and then people started voting. . . . He finished in ninth place and eleventh place.

—JON STEWART

Last week, during a speech to the NRA, Rudy Giuliani was interrupted by a cell phone call, which he stopped his speech to answer. Giuliani then told the audience, "That was my wife reminding me to pick up some milk at the 9-Eleven."

—SETH MEYERS

This kind of seems like bad taste to me. A Giuliani fund-raiser is now charging $9.11 in reference to 9/11. . . . Isn't that inappropriate? I mean, isn't it like a Bill Clinton fund-raiser charging $69 a head?

—JAY LENO

In footage that's already loosing shock value, doctors checked Saddam for lice and pronounced him a member of the Need a Bath Party.

—JON STEWART

The ability to joke about the wars reached fever pitch in May 2011, when we celebrated the death of bin Laden.

Bin Laden was buried at sea. Or, as Dick Cheney calls it, "the ultimate waterboarding."

—JAY LENO

Osama bin Laden is in the ocean. How ironic. Once again surrounded by seals.

—JAY LENO

The SEALs recovered an extensive stash of pornography from bin Laden's compound. It's probably not easy just having sex with the same eleven wives all the time. There were interesting titles: *Debby Does Abbottabad*, *Deep Goat*, *Bare Ankles 4*, and *Two Humps*, One *Camel*.

—JIMMY FALLON

Osama bin Laden had money and telephone numbers sewn into his clothes. Apparently we got him just as he was on his way to summer camp.

—JAY LENO

After all the talk about caves, bin Laden was hiding in a million-dollar mansion in Pakistan. The CIA became suspicious when they learned there was a million-dollar mansion in Pakistan.

—JIMMY KIMMEL

Osama bin Laden's death has been in the news all day. Leftish stations are going, "President Obama saves the world." Stations on the right are going, "Obama kills fellow Muslim."

—CRAIG FERGUSON

So for the most part, after September 11, late-night hosts followed this pattern: random jokes, patriotic jokes, and tangential event jokes, and then slowly went right at the topic.

It was long, slow joke foreplay. Except for Bill Maher. Right from the beginning he made it evident he was not going to change. Bill said, "I do not relinquish—nor should any of you— the right to criticize, even as we support, our government. This is still a democracy and they're still politicians, so we need to let our government know that we can't afford a lot of things that we used to be able to afford. Like a missile shield that will never work for an enemy that doesn't exist. We can't afford to be fighting wrong and silly wars. The cold war. The drug war. The culture war."

Then he said, "We have been the cowards. Lobbing cruise missiles from two thousand miles away. That's cowardly. Staying in the airplane when it hits the building. Say what you want about it. Not cowardly."

Even Al Qaeda leaders were going, *Oy vey*. Advertisers began boycotting, ABC stations dropped his show, and once again, a comment on a late-night show led to a White House response. Bush press secretary Ari Fleischer urged Americans to watch what they say.

But Bill's comment may actually have influenced the White House. ABC News later noted, "Maher's criticism may have been reiterated when President Bush warned Congress that the war on terrorism would be different than Kosovo: ground troops would be used. In other words, America is not a cruise missile–firing coward."

Eventually ABC dumped *Politically Incorrect* with Bill Maher, although it claimed the comment had nothing to do with it. Just like alcohol has nothing to do with topless selfies on spring break. Bill found a home at HBO and continues to be one of the sharpest, funniest, and most astute late-night hosts of all.

Shows that are on once a week like *SNL* and Bill Maher have an advantage—they have the luxury of time, they can spend an entire week developing their comedy, and also have time to see how a story plays out and if it is working on the other late-night shows. And at the end of the week, they can put a button on a story and sum it up. Those shows on every night have a different challenge. Jay, the Jimmys, and Dave have to guess at what will connect and try it out. If a topic and the jokes resonate, they can stay with them. Of course this has the critics saying, "They're beating the topic to death," but that's simply because they are hitting a good topic three or four nights in a row, while John Oliver, Bill Maher, and *SNL* are taking it on just one time after days of development. Jon Stewart and Stephen Colbert are truly amazing, for they are doing a nightly topical version of late night, yet one that doesn't rely on one-liners.

CHAPTER TWELVE

The Times They Are a-Changin'

Late-night comedy and what you can do on it have changed. It's still a constant battle. Sometimes there is a natural evolution and changing of standards as to what one can do on TV, sometimes there is the chilling effect of pressure groups. Fifty years ago Bill Dana could go on TV and do his "My name Jose Jimenez" routine; today if you use the words *illegal immigrants* in a joke instead of *undocumented workers*, people are outraged. The problem is that *undocumented workers* are great words for sociological studies, but not for a joke. They just don't have the impact and shorthand of the words *illegal immigrants*.

And for a lot of hosts, it's not worth the aggravation to get calls from the PC police and face the threat of lawsuits. On Leno we had a problem with jokes about Koreans and their fondness for eating dogs (over there, *101 Dalmatians* is dinner theater, and their Olive Garden serves penne poochenesca). Korean activists in LA protested that we were making fun of their culture. The way around it was to make the joke about "North Koreans," who are of course, not our friends.

The Sikh community was also upset at a bit we did in 2012. In that bit about the GOP presidential candidates' homes we showed the real-life homes of Ron Paul and Newt Gingrich. For Mitt Romney's home we showed a photo of the golden temple, which is the holiest site in the Sikh religion. To writers, this was a joke about Mitt's millions; the Sikh community was, yes, here is the word again, outraged, and sent a petition to NBC.

Jimmy Kimmel got in trouble in 2013 for a taped bit in which he asked a group of kids how to deal with the debt the United States owes China. One little boy said, "Kill everyone in China," and Kimmel said, "That's an interesting idea."

This blew up big-time with calls for ABC to fire Kimmel, numerous apologies, and demands from 1.3 billion outraged Chinese that if we didn't surrender Jimmy to their authorities, they would stop funding our national debt. If you want to know how seriously people take jokes, even the White House responded. We have a $17 trillion debt, troops overseas, and a crashing infrastructure, and somehow in the middle of the Obamacare website debacle, the White House took the time to say:

> The parties involved have already apologized independently. Jimmy Kimmel has apologized on air and issued a written apology. ABC has removed the skit from future broadcasts, taken the clip down from online platforms, and detailed several changes in its programming review process in response to this incident.

The president then noted that the First Amendment prevents the government from forcing Kimmel from the airwaves. The Chinese wanted to know why the government just couldn't run over Kimmel with a tank. Which is ridiculous. The Obama White House would have used drones. Or served him tainted North Korean dog.

And then Stephen Colbert got in trouble when he made a very smart and funny comment that was clearly meant to be anti-racist, and was accused of being racist. Colbert made fun of Redskins owner Daniel Snyder after he refused to change the name of his football team (he'd be better off changing the players) by saying that he would fund a group to support Native

Americans. Colbert went on Twitter to say, "I am willing to show the Asian community I care by introducing the Ching-Chong Ding-Dong Foundation for Sensitivity to Orientals or Whatever."

Again China wanted to send in the tanks, and as "punishment," Colbert was given *The Late Show* to host and a $5 million raise.

So comedy has evolved from the days of Mickey Rooney in *Breakfast at Tiffany's.* As Americans have become more PC, so have monologues, and everyone knows it is wrong to make fun of anyone because of where they are from. Unless they are French. Or Canadian. Or even better, French Canadian. Or are from a country that harbored, let's just say hypothetically, fifteen out of nineteen hijackers.

Thus, this joke by Jay caused no protests: "Saudi Arabia's highest religious council says allowing women to drive will end virginity. How bumpy are the roads in Saudi Arabia?"

Luckily there was no outrage from the Saudis or they may have secretly funded armed terrorists who would then attack us . . . Wait, they already did that.

The problem is that, despite our stated beliefs that all topics are fair game, the PC police have taken over. They are, on a daily basis, outraged. We are all outraged and offended at a joke. Everyone gets upset that someone's feelings were hurt.

Peyton Manning fans are upset that Terry Bradshaw said this: "Peyton Manning, considered the best quarterback to play the game today. Nobody would argue with that—if you like winning good during the season and losing Super Bowls, that's your guy."

Every joke has a target. Get over it, Manning fans.

LATE NIGHT VERSUS SOCIAL MEDIA

What do late-night writers think of social media? We hate it. We hate it the way Vladimir Putin hates wearing a shirt. We hate it because we used to be *the* source of jokes. Now everyone is a comic. Even worse, most are bad comics. There are now seven billion people who feel they can write a joke and 99 percent are not funny, or are racist, misogynist, anti-Semitic, or dumb, or just repeat something they heard from someone else. The other 1 percent—really funny.

And social media allows Joe Doakes to call and claim that Jay/Dave/Craig/the Jimmys/Whoever stole a joke. "Hello, late-night receptionist? Last night your host told a joke about Justin Bieber, and the day before I tweeted his name to my three followers, so one of your writers must have seen it and stolen it."

Here is my answer to Mr. Doakes. No, we didn't. No one

reads your tweets and no one checks out your Facebook page. What you did wasn't even a joke, and even if it was, there are obvious and identical jokes every pro writer is bound to do. They're the easy ones before we get to the ones we get paid way too much money for. Go back to your parents' basement.

Okay, now that I've vented again, let me say that deep down comedy writers love social media, because without it we never would have been able to know about Anthony Weiner's penis.

KNOW YOUR AUDIENCE

The landscape has changed for late night. I'm not bemoaning the change, I'm acknowledging it. Individual jokes that are quoted matter less; videos and bits that go viral on Fallon matter more. I'm still not convinced those translate to a larger viewership, which is the reason advertisers buy commercial ad time but make the shows hot, current, and trendy, and do influence TV audiences at home. You see Barack Obama slow-jam the news with Jimmy Fallon and you think he's cool. Or, as is more likely the case in 2015, you wonder why he's not working at his job. Either way, each and every late-night show matters in its own big or small way.

You have to know your audience. Jay's and Dave's audiences

are and were older people who are the offspring of those who watched Johnny. Jimmy Fallon's and Jimmy Kimmel's are younger viewers who get social media, the Internet, and going viral. Bill Maher's and Jon Stewart's are more political and ideological. I don't have any studies as a backup. It just seems true and logical. So those who write for those shows have to know their host and their audience.

And it's true not just of shows on at eleven p.m. I've been lucky enough to write for more than late night. Specifically, I've written for a number of awards shows and political speeches where people need to be funny: the Gridiron, the Inner Circle, the White House Correspondents' Association annual dinner, the Alfalfa Club dinner, the Al Smith Dinner, the South Boston St. Patrick's Day Breakfast Roast, the Congressional Correspondents Dinner.

The jokes may differ for those speeches but the principles remain the same:

> Know your audience.
> Don't try to sell them something they won't believe.
> Get them to like you up top . . . which for a
>   politician means being self-deprecating.
> Don't be needlessly mean.
> Be funny.

Thanks to being a *Tonight Show* writer I got to work with JFK Jr. In September 1996 I got a call from Paul Begala about writing for John. Paul was involved with *George* magazine, John had a big speech to do before a group from Nike, and Paul told him about his friend (me) at *The Tonight Show*. John had just gotten married and didn't know whether to address the group, and Paul suggested he talk to me. John called and we hit it off on the phone. My advice was to address the elephant in the room. So I gave him two lines, one referring to the fact that the day before Dennis Rodman had worn a wedding dress in public, and that the photo was everywhere on the news; the other had to do with Nike's slogan.

John opened his speech by saying that the night before his wedding he was worried about taking this big step. And it was Nike that came through. For as he looked out the window of his hotel room he saw a sign that said JUST DO IT. Big laughs. Remember, they are Nike officials. He then followed it by saying that he knew many in the audience had seen his wedding photos. And that his wife's wedding gown was one of only two like it in the world. The other was worn by Dennis Rodman.

Not brilliant jokes. We knew the audience, and although they were not killer jokes, they did in fact kill. Knowing the audience took a joke that was a five and made it into an eight. The next day there was a HUGE gift basket at the house; John called and hired me to write for *George* magazine. What an extraordinarily nice and fascinating person.

I also got to write for Santa Claus. I was writing a show for a televised Los Angeles Christmas tree lighting (yes, my motto is: no show too small, no fee too large) and the big finale had a surprise appearance of Santa Claus. The highlight came when Santa came to me and demanded that I put his lines on teleprompter to make sure he didn't forget them. So I wrote out these original and brilliant words for Santa and put them on the prompter: "Merry Christmas, Ho Ho Ho."

And they wonder why they have a reputation for being drunks.

CHAPTER THIRTEEN

After *The* Tonight Show

After twenty-two years with the best boss and the best show in my life, it's been hard to consider going elsewhere. I got some feelers from three late-night shows but the offers were like invites to the senior prom. "If Bob asks you to the prom, Cindy, would you consider it?" Maybe a better analogy is sex.

If you're married to the same person for twenty-two years, you know what she is like in bed. If you suddenly have to start dating again, there's a lot of angst over whether she'll like move number two, which was the old standby. My move number two involved batteries, but that's for another book. So, as of the writing of this book, I've been having fun doing awards shows. In the first three months after *The Tonight Show* was over I did the NAACP Image Awards, the Oscars, BET, the Academy of Country Music Awards, the Chaplin Award Gala, the American Comedy Awards, the All-Star Tribute to Don Rickles, the American Film Institute (AFI), the American Music Awards, and the Tonys. I also worked on a Senate campaign in Kentucky (once an addict, always an addict) and did some projects for Billy, Steve, Marty, and Chris Rock.

What has late night given me? I mean besides carpal tunnel syndrome and a condo in Boca? It's given me the chance to meet some really interesting people both at the show and as a result of my being a writer on the show. It's a nice comma, Jon Macks, *Tonight Show* writer; much better than Jon Macks, law school grad with a 2.5 GPA.

A few years ago Vice President Joe Biden was on *The Tonight Show*. I had done some debate prep for Joe, written some comedic remarks for him from time to time, and had even met him way back in 1986, when he did an event in Scranton for a gubernatorial candidate James Carville, Paul Begala, and I were working for. So when the vice president was done with the show, his staff called me upstairs and said, "Joe wants to say hi." I was of course dressed in my usual jeans, boots, and sloppy-ass T-shirt, so I grabbed a jacket I had stashed in the office for surprise occasions like this and went down. I saw Joe, we talked about the first time we had met (October 15, 1986—he is like Rain Man and Marilu Henner), then I started to go, saying, "Mr. Vice President, I know you're busy." Joe is, simply put, one of the most down-to-earth and "regular" guys I have ever met, and he wouldn't let me leave. We talked about the Eagles, the Phillies lineup, whether it was worth it for them to re-sign Jimmy Rollins, and then he invited me for dinner next time I was in DC. I thanked him and tried to leave. He wouldn't let me go. Twenty-five minutes later I finally got him to realize there were more important people than me to talk to and more important things to do. Like maybe Putin . . . or solving the federal debt. What a nice man.

In 2009 President Obama became the first sitting president to go on a late-night show. The producers made it clear, there would be no trying to meet him, and because of security we needed to stay in our offices. All good by me. Then, a few minutes before the show, there was a knock on the door and a staffer said, "The Secret Service wants to see you." Uh-oh. Maybe POTUS (that's president of the United States) wasn't happy with one of my jokes. The truth is, I had met Obama back in 2007, when David Axelrod had set up a meeting between the two of us. But back then he was a senator. Now he was the President with a capital P and that rhymes with C, which stands for commander-in-frigging-chief. So I was a little nervous. I went to the Secret Service agents and they said, "The president wants to see you." So they escorted me downstairs. During the thirty-second walk I'm trying to think of something clever to say. "How they hanging, Prez" didn't seem formal enough. So I went with what I knew would connect with him. We talked about the NCAA and my law school alma mater, Villanova. He thanked me for the work I had done for him in the past, especially for a joke I gave him when he first came on the show as a candidate. And before any Rs get upset, I have given jokes to President Bush and Laura Bush, too. All for comedy. On that show Jay had asked him how he felt about Hillary acting as if she were a shoo-in to get the nomination. It was the perfect setup for him to deliver the line I had sent to Axe. "It's not the first time a politician has declared 'mission accomplished' a little too soon."

We shook hands and I went back upstairs to write a dozen jokes about how badly he was screwing up the country.

I've gotten to meet some high-powered movie executives thanks to me being a comedy writer. Back in 2003 I was asked to do some punch-up on the movie *Looney Tunes: Back in Action*. The idea was to watch a screening of what they had put together and suggest funny lines. So I walked into a room with some studio executives who I sensed didn't quite know the movie franchise they had bought. I watched the film and then at the end submitted some lines, one of which was a line that Wile E. Coyote would have. He was hit by a boulder and then the sign would appear from under the rock with a line. At that point a thirty-year-old studio exec said, "But he's dead, how can he have a line?" Right then and there I knew I was not in the presence of Martin Scorsese–type genius.

Of course, being introduced as Jon Macks, *Tonight Show* writer, can cause problems. People expect you to "say something funny." They even expect me to tell them the best joke I ever wrote for Jay. I wrote 500,000. I think I remember three. And only because they got no laughs. The bar is set too high when someone introduces you as "really funny." Thus the incident with former British prime minister Tony Blair. I was in Washington, DC, a few years ago, having dinner with friends at Bourbon Steak. Across the room was John Kerry, having dinner with Tony Blair. I know the SOS (secretary of state) and didn't want to bother him. I'm not a political groupie, "Hey, introduce me to Tony." So I was having my dinner and getting progressively drunker. It doesn't take much. After about four hours of steak, two martinis, and a half bottle of wine, I staggered up to leave. As I did, the SOS saw me and waved me over. Great. Another time when I have to be clever. While drunk. When I got there, the SOS gave an effusive introduction about how brilliant a political strategist I used to be (note past tense) and how funny I am and then a big buildup about *The Tonight Show*. He ended by saying, "So, Tony, Jon is the funniest guy I know," and then he said, "And, Jon, this is Prime Minister Tony Blair." So I decided to try and be funny. The first thing that came to my mind was this. "I loved you in *The Queen*." Crickets. Nothing. A look of disdain. I staggered away. And that was only the first international incident I almost caused.

The second was in 2013. I was on the board of directors of the 100th Anniversary of Naval Aviation. Okay, you got me, I'm not an aviator. Since the celebration involved two produced programs, they wanted someone with show business experience to help. So Jonny the Joke Boy gets on the board. At the dinner celebrating the anniversary in Washington, DC, Prince Andrew was an honored guest. When I was introduced to him he was wearing a kilt, and all I could think about was the fact that for two months in the 1990s I did jokes about his then-wife, Fergie, getting her toes sucked by her boyfriend (Google it for the photos). Luckily I hadn't had a drink, so I was not going to bring up the aforementioned sucked toes. Instead, this sober exchange occurred.

THIRD PARTY: This is Jon Macks, he writes for *The Tonight Show*.

PRINCE ANDREW: [*Unintelligible noise.*]

JON: Hey [*pause*], this is awkward, but what do I call you, do I call you Andy or Prince Andrew?

PRINCE ANDREW: You can call me Your Royal Highness.

THIRD PARTY: Jon, don't!

JON: I thought we adjudicated that title back in 1776.

PRINCE ANDREW: [*Silence; sound of royal footsteps walking away.*]

The *Tonight Show* comma also got me dinner with Barbra Streisand. It wasn't direct but was a real bank shot, with my comedy comma getting me hired to write some AFI tributes, the tributes being seen by the people who run the Chaplin Award, who liked them, my getting hired to write the Chaplin Award Gala, where the award went to Barbra in 2013, and she liked what I wrote, and the offer coming for me to help her out a little with her upcoming world tour. But first she wanted to meet me. So it was May 2013, and the call comes as I am driving home that Barbra wants me to stop over at her house in Malibu for dinner. That night. In an hour. Who the fuck does she think she is? I have a life, I have plans, I'm an important person. So I canceled everything and said, "Yes."

I got to the main house and was ushered into a second house she has on the property called "Grandma's house" (why, I don't know), and was told to wait. She arrived looking fantastic. I wittily said, "Hi, Barbra, nice to meet you." She said, "That is the worst Philadelphia accent I have ever heard." I decided to throw deep. "Like your Brooklyn accent is understated." Silence for what seemed like an hour but was really 1/110th of a second. She laughed, we hit it off, and I got to work with one of the greatest singers of all time.

And the *Tonight Show* comma got me the chance to work with another singer, one who does an amazing impression of Streisand while not moving his lips! Terry Fator is a winner of *America's Got Talent* who went on to become the headliner at the Mirage in Las Vegas. He's a ventriloquist with an incredible talent—he has his puppets sing in the exact voices of everyone from Streisand to Garth Brooks to Nat King Cole to Taylor Swift. A once-in-a-lifetime talent. He was looking for new writers, the *Tonight Show* comma got him intrigued, and I started to write for Terry in 2011. He is the consummate total entertainer. Funny, can sing, great impressionist, an amazing show.

So there it is—Jon and the three Ps: politics, pop culture, and puppets. It's who I have been lucky enough to write for and about. So a book that began talking about how *The Tonight Show* and late-night shows affect all of us has ended with a story or two about how it affected my life. But it has not only given me that carpal and that Boca condo, late night has taught me some important things about life.

WHAT I LEARNED FROM LATE NIGHT

Here is what I've learned from monologue topics over the years:

> If you are going to tweet a picture of yourself, wear pants.
>
> In good times or bad there is always one sure way
> to become rich. Become a Wall Street CEO.
>
> If the pilot of your plane is seen carrying a case of
> tonic water and limes into the cockpit, get off.
>
> If you have no talent and want to become famous,
> make a sex tape.
>
> If you have talent, don't make a sex tape.
>
> Don't cheat with a woman more unattractive than
> your wife if you are named Prince Charles.
>
> If you are acquitted of a major crime, be thankful,
> hide from the public, and never try to get back
> your NFL memorabilia.
>
> If you are an actress under the age of thirty, try to
> not go commando when exiting a limo.
>
> If you are an actress over seventy, never go commando.
>
> Never insert a foreign-made cigar in a domestic-born
> intern.
>
> Don't say there are WMDs when there aren't any.

If you learn these lessons, you will pretty much have a great life.

POSTSCRIPT

So let me go back to those original questions from the beginning of the book.

Does anyone in late night (including this lowly writer) really have an impact on presidential elections? Yes, we can paint the canvas when it is blank and we can amplify what is out there about the person who is trying to hold the most important job in the world. In the end, you may not trust Fox News or MSNBC, but our late-night hosts do speak for us.

Are those jokes all of us have watched on late-night shows important? Important like the polio vaccine, no. Important in helping us relax and laugh after a bad day . . . yes.

Do we comedy writers matter in the larger sense? Or are all of us who write for late night just immature class clowns too unattractive to be stars in front of the camera? Yes.

Don't get me wrong. If I go back to late night, it's not because I believe I can change America with the power of a joke. Nor is it going to be for the money, although that doesn't hurt. It's because I love the daily challenge of writing a hundred jokes and seeing and hoping that a few score.

Obviously a lot of this book is based on my experience with Jay. Jay never wanted his jokes and commentary to change the world. He just wanted to make people laugh. In doing so, his jokes, like those of so many other hosts, have in fact had an impact far beyond what he dreamed. Maybe not to the extent that the single line of Tina's did about Sarah Palin's, but like all late-night comics, his jokes did shape our opinions. Jay always felt his jokes reflected what was already out there (the thermometer), but to me, regardless of whether it was Jay or anyone else with a late-night microphone, their jokes do influence the way we view events. They are a thermostat. Hey, without them, we might never know that O.J. was guilty.

So I owe my thanks to Johnny, who I watched growing up and who made me want to write comedy, and to Jay, who gave me that chance. Like I noted, 500,000 jokes and more to come. For those that made you laugh, I'm grateful; for those that made you groan, I apologize; for those that hurt people undeservedly, I feel bad; for those that helped you realize that a lot of celebrities and politicians are schmucks, I take credit; and for the chance to share them with you . . . my never-ending gratitude.

Years after Johnny left *The Tonight Show* his longtime friend Peter Lassally said, "The thing Johnny misses the most is the monologue. When he reads the paper every morning, he can think of five jokes off the bat that he wishes he has an outlet for."

I'm certainly not Johnny with an *h* but I get it. I'm lucky to have an outlet with the awards shows and comics I write for, but with the 2016 presidential race under way I can't help but look at the candidates and get comedy trigger finger. So in case I rejoin the late-night fray or for those who are in it now or are fans of the monologue, here is my alphabetical listing of the top 2016 political targets in the presidential or possible vice-presidential category with what you can expect jokes about. Note that some of them are so unknown or so unblemished, there is nothing to make fun of at this point in time: those would be Jim Webb, Elizabeth Warren and Martin O'Malley, John Kasich and Scott Walker.

2016ers

JOE BIDEN: Being vice president, will say anything, talks too long.

JEB BUSH: The dynasty, the first name.

CHRIS CHRISTIE: Temper, New Jersey, weight, and the fact he had more trouble with a bridge than Ted Kennedy.

HILLARY CLINTON: The dynasty, her being dead-broke when she left the White House, Benghazi.

TED CRUZ: He's Canadian, he's right-wing, he's crazy smart, and crazy; he wants to deport every Latino except himself.

ANDREW CUOMO: Dynasty; temper.

MIKE HUCKABEE: Name, Arkansas (a funny state), seems like a perennial loser.

RAND PAUL: College days, ophthalmology.

RICK SANTORUM: Sweaters, bigot, equates gay sex with man-on-dog sex (how does he know?).

BERNIE SANDERS: Eccentric gadfly.

FINAL THOUGHTS

ME AND MARIO

Seeing the passing of Mario Cuomo reminded me of the one time I met him. A truly amazing man and intellect, the tragedy wasn't that he never ran for president, the tragedy was that he never went on the Supreme Court. I would have loved to see him battle Scalia.

In 1989 I was doing the David Dinkins campaign for mayor against incumbent Ed Koch. We had debate prep (my first one) in the Sheraton. We had a suite and in it at various times were Dinkins, Bob Shrum, Bill Lynch, Harold Ickes, Harry Belafonte, and Mario Cuomo. Cuomo hated Koch and was doing everything he could to ensure Koch lost. And that meant lending his debate advice to Dinkins. One day during a break Cuomo wanders over to the window and yells, "Come here quick, but not you David." All of us ran over to the window to see what

Mario was looking at. He was looking at a woman in a window across the way, naked and toweling herself off after a shower. Brilliant politician that Cuomo was, he made sure Dinkins never came to the window to look, so he could have deniability. To this day I have no idea who the woman was, but she made debate prep a lot more fun than it ever was with any other candidate.

TOBY KEITH AND 2008

As part of the planning for the 2008 Democratic Convention I kept pushing for a country act. My idea was to have Garth Brooks and a black gospel choir sing "We Shall Be Free." I thought it would send a huge message about how Barack Obama was different, a break from the past, and that having a country connection would also be symbolic. Although Garth performed it months later at the inauguration, he couldn't make it to the convention so the campaign and I talked about other country stars who were Democrats. That's a smaller list than "Jewish sports heroes." Tim McGraw was one name that came up but he was on tour. Then one day the campaign called to ask me what I thought about Toby Keith. I'm a big Toby fan but killed that idea when I pointed out that it probably sent the wrong message if "End the war, Barack" had the star famous for the song "Courtesy of the Red, White and Blue (The Angry American)" with these lines:

'Cause we'll put a boot in your ass
It's the American way.

GEORGE JONES AND ME

In 1990 I made a music video. Well, actually not a music video, but a TV ad for Zell Miller when he ran for Georgia governor in 1990 that looked like a music video. Zell is the guy who got me my first pair of cowboy boots and is a big country fan. One day he called to say that the legendary George Jones was willing do to an ad. We came up with the idea that George would start singing "The Race Is On," then talk about how the race is on for governor and why he supported Zell. I flew to Nashville, got picked up by George's driver "PeeWee," went to the house, and had a lovely lunch with George and his wife, Nancy. We then went to shoot the ad. In the copy we had, George was to say, "And I'm for Zell because he is for a lottery for education, and boot camps for nonviolent drug offenders." I could see George was a little troubled as he did a few takes, so I called for a five-minute break and went over to him. He said, "Jon, I can't do that line." I said, "Why not?" He said, "Because I'm a nonviolent drug offender." We changed the line.

ACKNOWLEDGMENTS

On his deathbed, the actor Edmund Gwenn supposedly said, "Dying is easy, comedy is hard." Let me change that to "Writing a book is easy, deciding who gets acknowledged is hard." Nevertheless, here goes.

To David Rosenthal and Sarah Hochman at Blue Rider Press. They are brilliant, patient, willing to put up with my deadline lies, and helped shape this book and bring it to life.

To my wife, Julie, and kids Daniel, Samantha, and Ricky, who put up with me closing the door and yelling, "Leave me alone, I have to finish this book."

To the friends, political buddies, and fellow comedy writers who read the early drafts and helped me not make too big a fool of myself: John Romeo, David Wade, Dave Boone, and Paul Begala.

To my manager, David Steinberg, for his friendship, guidance, and for always encouraging me to take on new challenges.

To my agents at WME, Evan Warner and Mel Berger, who took this idea from day one and made it happen.

To the comics who make me laugh and who have given me the privilege of working for them: Billy Crystal, Marty Short, Steve Martin, and Chris Rock.

To the best Oscar producer of all time, Gil Cates.

To friends like Barry Adelman, Jerry Colbert, Ken Erlich, Terry Fator, Bob Gazzale, Phil Gurin, Juliane Hare, Charlie Haykel, Reggie Hudlin, John Irwin, Brad Lachman, and Don Mischer, who have given me so many great opportunities above and beyond writing monologue jokes.

To TV and film producer Mark Sennet, who is also a great photographer and took the photo of me on this book's cover.

And to Jay Leno for giving me a new career back in 1992, and to all the late-night hosts. Thanks for the laughs.